Fraction

Turn to each section to find a more detailed skills list.

Table of Contents

What Does This Book Include?

- More than 80 student practice pages that build basic fraction skills
- A detailed skills list for each section of the book
- Send-home letters informing parents of the skills being targeted and ways to practice these skills
- Student checkups
- A reproducible student progress chart
- Awards to celebrate student progress
- Answer keys for easy checking
- Perforated pages for easy removal and filing if desired

What Are the Benefits of This Book?

- Organized for quick and easy use
- Enhances and supports your existing math program
- Offers approximately four reproducible practice pages for each basic fraction skill
- Helps develop mastery of fraction skills
- Provides reinforcement for different ability levels
- Includes communication pages that encourage parent participation in the child's learning of math
- Contains checkups that assess students' fraction knowledge
- Offers a reproducible chart for documenting student progress
- Aligns with national math standards

©2004 by THE EDUCATION CENTER, INC.
All rights reserved.
ISBN# 1-56234-544-3

Manufactured in the United States
10 9 8 7 6 5 4 3 2

How to Use This Book
Steps to Success

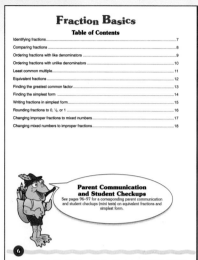

Choose Skills to Target

Scan the detailed table of contents at the beginning of each section to find just the right skills to target your students' needs.

Select Fun Practice Pages

From a variety of fun formats, choose the pages that best match your students' current ability levels.

Fun Formats

Date Skill Completed

Targeted Skill

Letter to Parents Informing Them of Skill to Review

Problems for Practice

Communicate With Parents

Recruit parent assistance by locating the appropriate parent letter (pages 96–122), making copies, and sending the letter home.

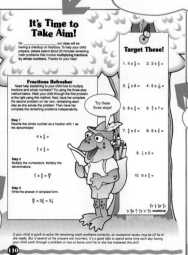

Fraction Review for Parents

Assess Student Understanding

Assess students' progress with student checkups (mini tests) on pages 97–123.

Checkup 8

Name _____ Date _____

A. $\frac{1}{3} \times 5 =$ $7 \times \frac{6}{7} =$ $6 \times \frac{1}{8} =$

B. $3 \times \frac{4}{9} =$ $\frac{5}{6} \times 8 =$ $4 \times \frac{1}{6} =$

C. $\frac{3}{4} \times 2 =$ $3 \times \frac{3}{10} =$

D. $\frac{2}{9} \times 5 =$ $4 \times \frac{3}{4} =$

Test A: Multiplying fractions by whole numbers

Checkup 8

Name _____ Date _____

A. $4 \times \frac{1}{8} =$ $\frac{3}{5} \times 5 =$ $8 \times \frac{1}{10} =$

B. $\frac{5}{7} \times 7 =$ $3 \times \frac{4}{5} =$ $6 \times \frac{1}{6} =$

C. $\frac{5}{8} \times 4 =$ $9 \times \frac{2}{5} =$

D. $6 \times \frac{1}{2} =$ $\frac{1}{4} \times 10 =$

Test B: Multiplying fractions by whole numbers

Specific Skills Tested

Document Progress

Documenting student progress can be as easy as 1, 2, 3! Do the following for each student:

1. Make a copy of the student progress chart (pages 124–125).
2. File the chart in his math portfolio or a class notebook.
3. Record the date each checkup is given, the number of correct answers, and any comments regarding his progress.

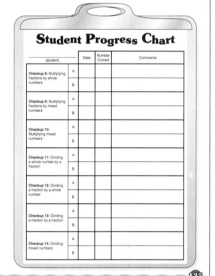

Student Progress Chart

(student)		Date	Number Correct	Comments
Checkup 8: Multiplying fractions by whole numbers	A			
	B			
Checkup 9: Multiplying fractions by mixed numbers	A			
	B			
Checkup 10: Multiplying mixed numbers	A			
	B			
Checkup 11: Dividing a whole number by a fraction	A			
	B			
Checkup 12: Dividing a fraction by a whole number	A			
	B			
Checkup 13: Dividing a fraction by a fraction	A			
	B			
Checkup 14: Dividing mixed numbers	A			
	B			

125

Celebrate!

Celebrate fraction success using the awards on page 95.

You Hit the Bull's-Eye!

_____

has mastered **multiplying and dividing fractions.**

_____
Teacher

_____
Date

3

Books in the Target Math Success series include

- *Basic Addition Facts to 18*
- *Basic Subtraction Facts to 18*
- *Addition of Larger Numbers*
- *Subtraction of Larger Numbers*
- *Basic Multiplication Facts and More*
- *Basic Division Facts and More*
- *Multiplication of Larger Numbers*
- *Division of Larger Numbers*
- *Fractions*
- *Decimals*

Managing Editor: Peggy W. Hambright
Editor at Large: Diane Badden
Staff Editors: Lauren E. Cox, Debra Liverman, Sherry McGregor
Copy Editors: Tazmen Carlisle, Amy Kirtley-Hill, Karen L. Mayworth, Kristy Parton, Debbie Shoffner, Cathy Edwards Simrell
Cover Artist: Kimberly Richard
Art Coordinator: Pam Crane
Artists: Pam Crane, Theresa Lewis Goode, Clevell Harris, Ivy L. Koonce, Clint Moore, Greg D. Rieves, Rebecca Saunders, Barry Slate, Stuart Smith, Donna K. Teal
The Mailbox® Books.com: Judy P. Wyndham (MANAGER); Jennifer Tipton Bennett (DESIGNER/ARTIST); Karen White (INTERNET COORDINATOR); Paul Fleetwood, Xiaoyun Wu (SYSTEMS)

President, The Mailbox Book Company™: Joseph C. Bucci
Director of Book Planning and Development: Chris Poindexter
Curriculum Director: Karen P. Shelton
Book Development Managers: Cayce Guiliano, Elizabeth H. Lindsay, Thad McLaurin
Editorial Planning: Kimberley Bruck (MANAGER); Debra Liverman, Sharon Murphy, Susan Walker (TEAM LEADERS)
Editorial and Freelance Management: Karen A. Brudnak; Sarah Hamblet, Hope Rodgers (EDITORIAL ASSISTANTS)
Editorial Production: Lisa K. Pitts (TRAFFIC MANAGER); Lynette Dickerson (TYPE SYSTEMS); Mark Rainey (TYPESETTER)
Librarian: Dorothy C. McKinney

www.themailbox.com

Fraction Basics

Table of Contents

Parent Communication and Student Checkups

See pages 96–97 for a corresponding parent communication and student checkups (mini tests) on equivalent fractions and simplest form.

Sweet Dreams!

Name _____ Date _____

Write the fraction shown.
Cross off the matching answer on the bear's blanket.
Some answers will not be crossed off.

_____

_____

_____

_____

_____

_____

_____

_____

$$\frac{7}{10} \qquad \frac{4}{9} \qquad \frac{9}{14} \qquad \frac{13}{16}$$

$$\frac{1}{4} \qquad \frac{3}{8} \qquad \frac{1}{6} \qquad \frac{8}{15} \qquad \frac{5}{12} \qquad \frac{4}{5}$$

Saturn's Rings?

Name _____ Date _____

Compare the fractions.
Write <, >, or =.
Color by the code.

$\frac{1}{3} \bigcirc \frac{1}{2}$

$\frac{3}{4} \bigcirc \frac{1}{2}$

$\frac{6}{10} \bigcirc \frac{3}{5}$

$\frac{4}{16} \bigcirc \frac{1}{4}$

$\frac{1}{4} \bigcirc \frac{1}{5}$

$\frac{1}{4} \bigcirc \frac{2}{3}$

$\frac{2}{5} \bigcirc \frac{2}{3}$

$\frac{2}{3} \bigcirc \frac{3}{4}$

$\frac{1}{5} \bigcirc \frac{3}{15}$

$\frac{1}{7} \bigcirc \frac{1}{8}$

$\frac{3}{5} \bigcirc \frac{3}{4}$

$\frac{6}{9} \bigcirc \frac{1}{2}$

$\frac{5}{7} \bigcirc \frac{3}{8}$

$\frac{5}{8} \bigcirc \frac{3}{4}$

$\frac{1}{3} \bigcirc \frac{2}{6}$

$\frac{5}{8} \bigcirc \frac{7}{12}$

$\frac{1}{6} \bigcirc \frac{2}{8}$

$\frac{3}{4} \bigcirc \frac{6}{8}$

Comparing fractions

©The Education Center, Inc. • *Target Math Success* • TEC60833 • Key p. 127

Extra Sharp Cheese

Name _____ Date _____

Order each set of fractions from least to greatest.
To answer the riddle, write the letter of the corresponding fraction in each box.
The first one has been done for you.

When does a piece of cheese become an artist?

K	T	W
$\frac{2}{9}$,	$\frac{7}{9}$,	$\frac{4}{9}$

$\frac{2}{9}$, $\frac{4}{9}$, $\frac{7}{9}$

___ , ___ , $\boxed{W}$

E	Q	H
$\frac{4}{5}$,	$\frac{3}{5}$,	$\frac{2}{5}$

___ , ___ , ___

☐ , ☐

E	N	R
$\frac{3}{7}$,	$\frac{5}{7}$,	$\frac{2}{7}$

___ , ___ , ___

☐

T	Z	I
$\frac{7}{8}$,	$\frac{1}{8}$,	$\frac{2}{8}$

___ , ___ , ___

☐ ☐

V	R	D
$\frac{7}{10}$,	$\frac{3}{10}$,	$\frac{1}{10}$

___ , ___ , ___

☐ ☐

W	A	S
$\frac{7}{16}$,	$\frac{3}{16}$,	$\frac{11}{16}$

___ , ___ , ___

☐ ☐ ☐

C	M	K
$\frac{5}{12}$,	$\frac{1}{12}$,	$\frac{11}{12}$

___ , ___ , ___

☐

B	A	I
$\frac{14}{15}$,	$\frac{1}{15}$,	$\frac{4}{15}$

___ , ___ , ___

☐

E	X	C
$\frac{7}{11}$,	$\frac{5}{11}$,	$\frac{2}{11}$

___ , ___ , ___

☐ ☐!

Ordering fractions with like denominators

Ant Farm?

Name _____   Date _____

Order each set of fractions from least to greatest.
Show your work on another sheet of paper.
Color if correct to show the path to the two workers.

Start

$\dfrac{1}{4}$, $\dfrac{1}{2}$, $\dfrac{5}{6}$

$\dfrac{1}{6}$, $\dfrac{1}{8}$, $\dfrac{2}{3}$

$\dfrac{3}{7}$, $\dfrac{1}{2}$, $\dfrac{3}{4}$

$\dfrac{3}{10}$, $\dfrac{2}{3}$, $\dfrac{4}{5}$

$\dfrac{1}{6}$, $\dfrac{2}{9}$, $\dfrac{1}{3}$

$\dfrac{7}{8}$, $\dfrac{2}{9}$, $\dfrac{1}{3}$

$\dfrac{4}{5}$, $\dfrac{9}{10}$, $\dfrac{11}{12}$

$\dfrac{1}{2}$, $\dfrac{1}{8}$, $\dfrac{1}{7}$

$\dfrac{7}{12}$, $\dfrac{3}{10}$, $\dfrac{1}{5}$

$\dfrac{3}{8}$, $\dfrac{9}{10}$, $\dfrac{1}{4}$

$\dfrac{2}{3}$, $\dfrac{5}{7}$, $\dfrac{7}{9}$

$\dfrac{3}{8}$, $\dfrac{3}{5}$, $\dfrac{7}{10}$

$\dfrac{3}{4}$, $\dfrac{1}{2}$, $\dfrac{11}{16}$

$\dfrac{6}{7}$, $\dfrac{2}{3}$, $\dfrac{5}{6}$

$\dfrac{1}{3}$, $\dfrac{5}{9}$, $\dfrac{7}{18}$

$\dfrac{1}{3}$, $\dfrac{2}{5}$, $\dfrac{1}{2}$

$\dfrac{5}{8}$, $\dfrac{7}{16}$, $\dfrac{3}{4}$

$\dfrac{3}{4}$, $\dfrac{2}{5}$, $\dfrac{13}{16}$

$\dfrac{9}{14}$, $\dfrac{4}{7}$, $\dfrac{3}{4}$

$\dfrac{1}{6}$, $\dfrac{1}{5}$, $\dfrac{2}{9}$

10 Ordering fractions with unlike denominators

Which Pizza?

Find the least common multiple.
Color to show the path to the pizza.

3 and 4	12	8	6	16
2 and 5	5	10	15	4
7 and 9	16	56	63	126
3 and 8	8	12	24	16
2 and 4	2	8	6	4
3 and 9	27	18	9	3
4 and 5	15	20	40	30
2 and 6	3	6	12	16
9 and 4	36	24	40	13
12 and 3	4	12	36	15
6 and 8	48	36	24	32
2 and 7	7	24	21	14
6 and 10	10	60	16	30
8 and 5	20	45	40	50
3 and 6	3	6	9	18
5 and 7	35	30	12	45
8 and 12	24	12	8	4
4 and 6	24	12	36	48

mushrooms   papaya   peppers   pineapple

H₂O Humor

Name _____   Date _____

Circle the equivalent fraction.
To solve the riddle, match the letter to the
    equivalent fraction on the right.
The first one has been done for you.

When does water stop running downhill?

$\dfrac{W}{}$						
$\dfrac{6}{18}$	$\dfrac{4}{6}$	$\dfrac{36}{42}$	$\dfrac{14}{35}$		$\dfrac{21}{24}$	$\dfrac{12}{32}$
$\dfrac{9}{12}$	$\dfrac{9}{15}$	$\dfrac{20}{32}$	$\dfrac{3}{8}$	$\dfrac{4}{8}$	$\dfrac{6}{7}$	$\dfrac{19}{38}$
			$\dfrac{5}{6}$	$\dfrac{16}{24}$	$\dfrac{8}{12}$	
$\dfrac{5}{20}$	$\dfrac{2}{3}$	$\dfrac{25}{30}$	$\dfrac{10}{20}$	$\dfrac{22}{30}$	$\dfrac{6}{8}$	

$\dfrac{1}{3} =$

(circled) $\dfrac{6}{18}$ **W** $\dfrac{2}{5}$ **S**

$\dfrac{2}{4} =$

$\dfrac{6}{8}$ **L** $\dfrac{4}{8}$ **H**

$\dfrac{5}{6} =$

$\dfrac{25}{30}$ **T** $\dfrac{20}{30}$ **M**

$\dfrac{2}{3} =$

$\dfrac{8}{12}$ **E** $\dfrac{6}{15}$ **A**

$\dfrac{3}{5} =$

$\dfrac{6}{15}$ **G** $\dfrac{9}{15}$ **E**

$\dfrac{10}{12} =$

$\dfrac{5}{6}$ **T** $\dfrac{3}{4}$ **C**

$\dfrac{3}{8} =$

$\dfrac{15}{30}$ **K** $\dfrac{12}{32}$ **T**

$\dfrac{6}{7} =$

$\dfrac{36}{42}$ **E** $\dfrac{24}{27}$ **U**

$\dfrac{5}{8} =$

$\dfrac{10}{24}$ **B** $\dfrac{20}{32}$ **A**

$\dfrac{2}{4} =$

$\dfrac{4}{6}$ **D** $\dfrac{10}{20}$ **T**

$\dfrac{4}{6} =$

$\dfrac{16}{24}$ **H** $\dfrac{8}{16}$ **P**

$\dfrac{2}{5} =$

$\dfrac{14}{35}$ **N** $\dfrac{10}{10}$ **F**

$\dfrac{1}{2} =$

$\dfrac{19}{38}$ **S** $\dfrac{18}{38}$ **V**

$\dfrac{3}{4} =$

$\dfrac{9}{16}$ **J** $\dfrac{6}{8}$ **M**

$\dfrac{7}{8} =$

$\dfrac{15}{16}$ **Q** $\dfrac{21}{24}$ **I**

$\dfrac{42}{49} =$

$\dfrac{6}{7}$ **E** $\dfrac{6}{6}$ **Y**

$\dfrac{1}{4} =$

$\dfrac{3}{8}$ **A** $\dfrac{5}{20}$ **B**

$\dfrac{11}{15} =$

$\dfrac{22}{30}$ **O** $\dfrac{33}{55}$ **C**

$\dfrac{2}{3} =$

$\dfrac{4}{5}$ **E** $\dfrac{4}{6}$ **H**

$\dfrac{6}{9} =$

$\dfrac{1}{3}$ **H** $\dfrac{2}{3}$ **O**

$\dfrac{15}{40} =$

$\dfrac{3}{8}$ **C** $\dfrac{30}{40}$ **N**

$\dfrac{27}{36} =$

$\dfrac{3}{12}$ **L** $\dfrac{9}{12}$ **R**

Equivalent fractions

Bear Hair

Name _____ Date _____

Circle the correct set of factors for each number.
Write the greatest common factor for each pair of numbers in the box.

What does a bear
wear in her hair?

1. **3:** 1, 3 or 1, 2, 3
   6: 1, 2, 3, 4, 6 or 1, 2, 3, 6

   GCF: ☐
   E

2. **4:** 1, 2, 3, 4 or 1, 2, 4
   8: 1, 2, 4, 8 or 1, 8

   GCF: ☐
   A

3. **10:** 1, 2, 4, 5, 6, 10 or 1, 2, 5, 10
   20: 1, 2, 4, 5, 10, 20 or 1, 10, 10, 70

   GCF: ☐
   E

4. **16:** 1, 4, 16 or 1, 2, 4, 8, 16
   32: 1, 2, 4, 8, 16, 32 or 1, 4, 8, 32

   GCF: ☐
   T

5. **6:** 1, 6 or 1, 2, 3, 6
   12: 1, 2, 6, 12 or 1, 2, 3, 4, 6, 12

   GCF: ☐
   B

6. **4:** 1, 2, 4 or 1, 2, 3, 4
   14: 1, 2, 7 or 1, 2, 7, 14

   GCF: ☐
   E

7. **28:** 1, 4, 7, 28 or 1, 2, 4, 7, 14, 28
   35: 1, 5, 7, 35 or 1, 2, 5, 7, 17, 35

   GCF: ☐
   T

8. **18:** 1, 3, 6, 18 or 1, 2, 3, 6, 9, 18
   27: 1, 3, 9, 27 or 1, 3, 4, 7, 9, 27

   GCF: ☐
   R

To solve the riddle, match the letters above to the numbered lines below.

A " ___ ___ ___ - ___ ___ ___ ___ "
     6   2   4   9   10   16   7   3

Sneaking Some Snacks

Name _____ Date _____

Match each fraction to its simplest form.
Color each pair of equivalent fractions the same color.

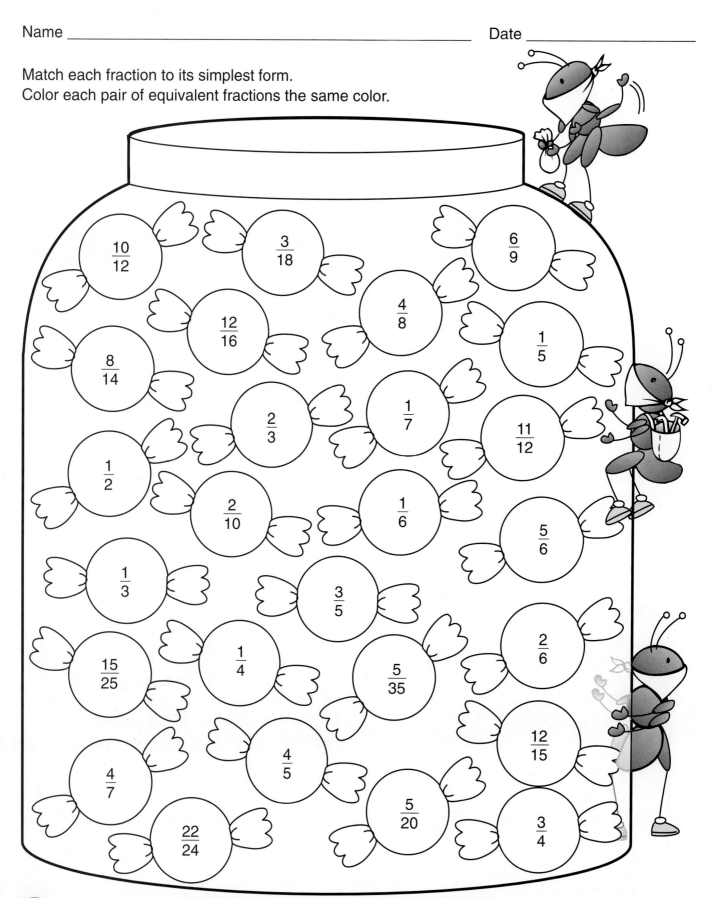

Finding the simplest form

Power Practice

Name _____ Date _____

Write each fraction in simplest form.

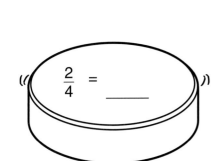

$\frac{2}{4} = $ _____

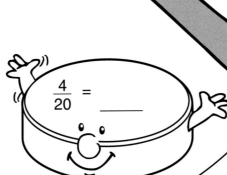

$\frac{4}{20} = $ _____

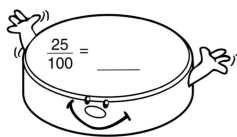

$\frac{25}{100} = $ _____

$\frac{3}{6} = $ _____

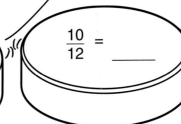

$\frac{10}{12} = $ _____

$\frac{3}{9} = $ _____

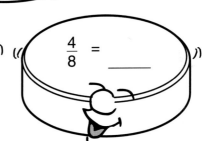

$\frac{4}{8} = $ _____

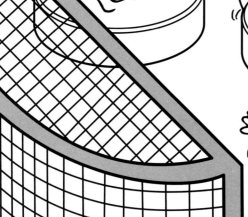

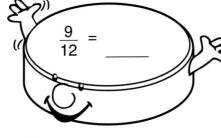

$\frac{9}{12} = $ _____

$\frac{6}{8} = $ _____

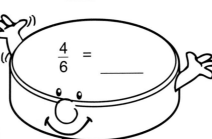

$\frac{4}{6} = $ _____

$\frac{10}{25} = $ _____

Quilting Bees

Name _____ Date _____

Round each fraction to 0, $\frac{1}{2}$, or 1.
The first one has been done for you.
Color by the code.

Color Code

0	=	purple
$\frac{1}{2}$	=	yellow
1	=	green

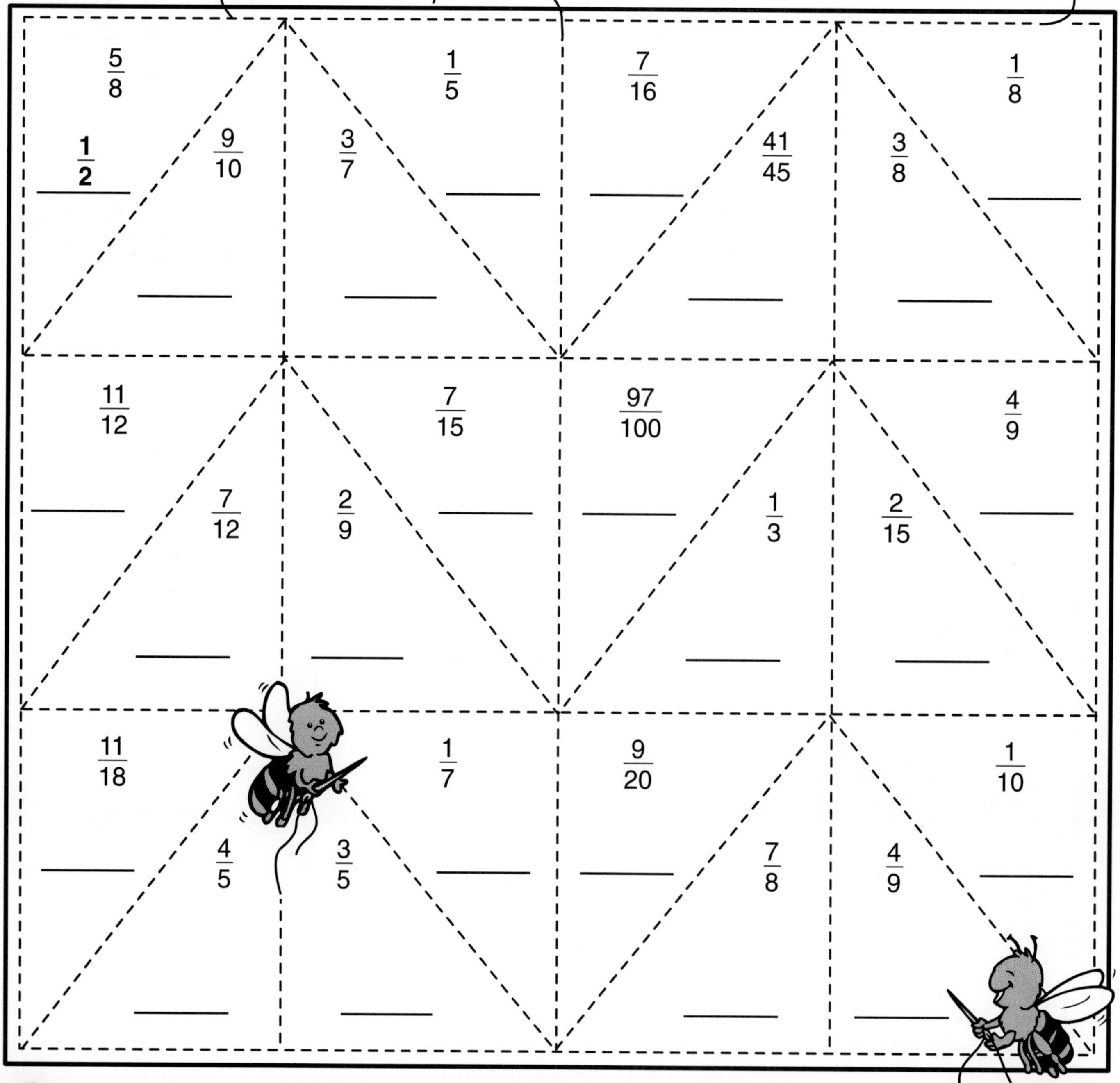

$\frac{5}{8}$

$\frac{1}{5}$

$\frac{7}{16}$

$\frac{1}{8}$

$\frac{1}{2}$

$\frac{9}{10}$

$\frac{3}{7}$

$\frac{41}{45}$

$\frac{3}{8}$

$\frac{11}{12}$

$\frac{7}{15}$

$\frac{97}{100}$

$\frac{4}{9}$

$\frac{7}{12}$

$\frac{2}{9}$

$\frac{1}{3}$

$\frac{2}{15}$

$\frac{11}{18}$

$\frac{1}{7}$

$\frac{9}{20}$

$\frac{1}{10}$

$\frac{4}{5}$

$\frac{3}{5}$

$\frac{7}{8}$

$\frac{4}{9}$

Chicken on a Mission

Name _____   Date _____

Rename each improper fraction as a mixed number in simplest form.
Cross off the answer on the french fry box.
Some numbers will not be crossed off.

$\frac{54}{7} =$ $\frac{24}{9} =$ $\frac{13}{3} =$

$\frac{49}{7} =$ $\frac{15}{8} =$ $\frac{37}{2} =$

$\frac{14}{5} =$ $\frac{18}{4} =$ $\frac{72}{9} =$ $\frac{58}{10} =$

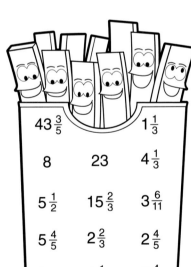

French fry box answers:

$43\frac{3}{5}$		$1\frac{1}{3}$
8	23	$4\frac{1}{3}$
$5\frac{1}{2}$	$15\frac{2}{3}$	$3\frac{6}{11}$
$5\frac{4}{5}$	$2\frac{2}{3}$	$2\frac{4}{5}$
3	$4\frac{1}{2}$	$9\frac{4}{5}$
$18\frac{1}{2}$	7	$1\frac{7}{8}$
$7\frac{5}{7}$	$9\frac{3}{5}$	$5\frac{1}{6}$

$\frac{62}{12} =$ $\frac{48}{5} =$ $\frac{12}{4} =$

$\frac{44}{8} =$ $\frac{47}{3} =$ $\frac{12}{9} =$

Two of a Kind

Name _____   Date _____

Read the numbers on the first spider.
Color each matching pair of shoes a different color.
Repeat for the remaining three spiders.

Adding Fractions

Table of Contents

Parent Communication and Student Checkups

See pages 98–103 for corresponding parent communications and student checkups (mini tests) for the skills listed above.

Up, Up, and Away!

Name _____   Date _____

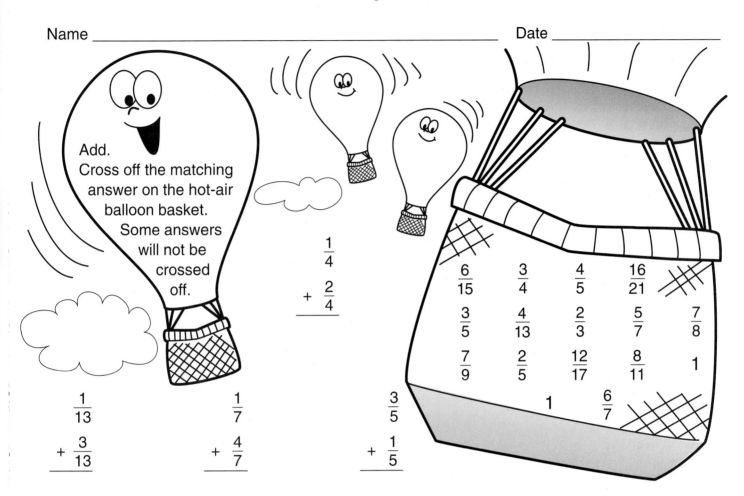

Add.
Cross off the matching answer on the hot-air balloon basket.
Some answers will not be crossed off.

$$\frac{1}{4} + \frac{2}{4}$$

Balloon basket answers:

$\frac{6}{15}$	$\frac{3}{4}$	$\frac{4}{5}$	$\frac{16}{21}$	
$\frac{3}{5}$	$\frac{4}{13}$	$\frac{2}{3}$	$\frac{5}{7}$	$\frac{7}{8}$
$\frac{7}{9}$	$\frac{2}{5}$	$\frac{12}{17}$	$\frac{8}{11}$	1
		1	$\frac{6}{7}$	

$$\frac{1}{13} + \frac{3}{13}$$

$$\frac{1}{7} + \frac{4}{7}$$

$$\frac{3}{5} + \frac{1}{5}$$

$$\frac{2}{9} + \frac{5}{9}$$

$$\frac{1}{3} + \frac{1}{3}$$

$$\frac{2}{5} + \frac{1}{5}$$

$$\frac{3}{8} + \frac{5}{8}$$

$$\frac{2}{7} + \frac{4}{7}$$

$$\frac{10}{21} + \frac{6}{21}$$

$$\frac{3}{11} + \frac{5}{11}$$

$$\frac{7}{17} + \frac{5}{17}$$

$$\frac{4}{15} + \frac{2}{15}$$

$$\frac{5}{6} + \frac{1}{6}$$

Adding fractions with like denominators

Your Turn, Mate!

Add.
Color if correct to show the path back to the thrower.

$$\frac{2}{7} + \frac{4}{7} = \frac{6}{7}$$

$$\frac{3}{4} + \frac{1}{4} = 1$$

$$\frac{1}{3} + \frac{2}{3} = \frac{3}{6}$$

$$\frac{4}{9} + \frac{2}{9} = \frac{2}{3}$$

$$\frac{1}{10} + \frac{7}{10} = \frac{4}{5}$$

$$\frac{5}{11} + \frac{7}{11} = \frac{12}{22}$$

$$\frac{7}{13} + \frac{9}{13} = 1\frac{3}{13}$$

$$\frac{7}{12} + \frac{9}{12} = \frac{16}{24}$$

$$\frac{5}{8} + \frac{1}{8} = \frac{3}{4}$$

$$\frac{2}{3} + \frac{2}{3} = \frac{3}{4}$$

$$\frac{5}{8} + \frac{3}{8} = 1$$

$$\frac{3}{5} + \frac{4}{5} = \frac{7}{10}$$

$$\frac{4}{7} + \frac{6}{7} = \frac{9}{7}$$

$$\frac{7}{10} + \frac{9}{10} = 1\frac{3}{5}$$

$$\frac{3}{5} + \frac{1}{5} = \frac{4}{10}$$

$$\frac{8}{15} + \frac{6}{15} = \frac{14}{15}$$

$$\frac{8}{15} + \frac{2}{15} = \frac{2}{3}$$

It's coming back!

Adding fractions with like denominators

A Better Birdhouse

Name _____ Date _____

Add.
Write the answer in simplest form.

$\frac{2}{5} + \frac{1}{5} =$

$\frac{3}{7} + \frac{2}{7} =$

$\frac{5}{9} + \frac{1}{9} =$

$\frac{1}{4} + \frac{3}{4} =$

$\frac{5}{12} + \frac{5}{12} =$

$\frac{7}{20} + \frac{3}{20} =$

$\frac{1}{3} + \frac{1}{3} =$

$\frac{4}{15} + \frac{9}{15} =$

$\frac{3}{8} + \frac{5}{8} =$

$\frac{5}{14} + \frac{3}{14} =$

$\frac{3}{10} + \frac{7}{10} =$

$\frac{3}{8} + \frac{3}{8} =$

$\frac{4}{11} + \frac{6}{11} =$

$\frac{2}{9} + \frac{4}{9} =$

$\frac{6}{15} + \frac{4}{15} =$

$\frac{5}{16} + \frac{7}{16} =$

$\frac{2}{7} + \frac{4}{7} =$

$\frac{1}{6} + \frac{5}{6} =$

$\frac{1}{3} + \frac{2}{3} =$

$\frac{3}{5} + \frac{1}{5} =$

$\frac{1}{8} + \frac{3}{8} =$

$\frac{4}{9} + \frac{5}{9} =$

$\frac{5}{10} + \frac{1}{10} =$

Adding fractions with like denominators **23**

"Fan-tastic" Concert

Name _____   Date _____

Read.
Solve each problem on another sheet of paper.
Write the answer in simplest form in the blank.

1. By 5:00 P.M. $\frac{1}{8}$ of the concert crowd had arrived. By 6:00 P.M., another $\frac{5}{8}$ had arrived. What fraction of the concert crowd had arrived by 6:00 P.M.?

_____ of the concert crowd

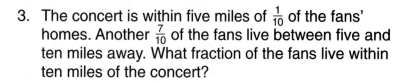

2. Before the show, $\frac{3}{7}$ of the fans bought their tickets online and $\frac{3}{7}$ bought them over the phone. What fraction of the fans bought their tickets either online or over the phone?

_____ of the fans

3. The concert is within five miles of $\frac{1}{10}$ of the fans' homes. Another $\frac{7}{10}$ of the fans live between five and ten miles away. What fraction of the fans live within ten miles of the concert?

_____ of the fans

4. For $\frac{1}{4}$ of the fans, this is their first concert. Another $\frac{1}{4}$ have been to one other concert. What fraction of the fans have only been to one or two concerts?

_____ of the fans

5. The No-Man Band has played $\frac{2}{3}$ of its scheduled concerts. It will play $\frac{1}{3}$ of its concerts during the next three weeks. What fraction of its concerts will the band have played in three weeks?

_____ of the band's concerts

6. The band played $\frac{2}{5}$ of its hit songs before intermission. It played $\frac{1}{5}$ of its hits afterward. How many of its hit songs did the No-Man Band play in all?

_____ of its hit songs

Story problems: adding fractions with like denominators

Polar Beach

Name _____ Date _____

Add.
Show your work.
Write the answer in simplest form.
Cross off the answer on the lifeguard chair.
Some numbers will not be crossed off.

$\dfrac{1}{2}$

$+ \dfrac{1}{4}$

$\dfrac{1}{6}$

$+ \dfrac{3}{8}$

$\dfrac{7}{12}$

$+ \dfrac{1}{3}$

$\dfrac{7}{8}$

$+ \dfrac{1}{9}$

$\dfrac{4}{11}$

$+ \dfrac{1}{2}$

$\dfrac{1}{6}$

$+ \dfrac{1}{9}$

$\dfrac{1}{6}$

$+ \dfrac{2}{3}$

$\dfrac{3}{10}$

$+ \dfrac{2}{5}$

$\dfrac{1}{4}$

$+ \dfrac{1}{8}$

$\dfrac{2}{5}$

$+ \dfrac{4}{9}$

$\dfrac{4}{5}$

$+ \dfrac{1}{10}$

$\dfrac{3}{8}$

$+ \dfrac{9}{16}$

$\dfrac{14}{19}$	$\dfrac{5}{18}$	$\dfrac{38}{45}$
$\dfrac{15}{16}$	$\dfrac{5}{6}$ $\dfrac{12}{24}$	$\dfrac{71}{72}$
$\dfrac{3}{4}$	$\dfrac{19}{22}$ $\dfrac{7}{10}$	$\dfrac{9}{10}$
$\dfrac{3}{8}$		$\dfrac{11}{12}$
	$\dfrac{13}{24}$	

NO DIVING

Adding fractions with unlike denominators

Homeward Bound

Name _____   Date _____

Follow the directions below to help Alvin Alien find his way home.
Add.
Show your work on another sheet of paper.
Write the answer in simplest form.
Color the answer to show the path
   to the planet.

$\frac{1}{5} + \frac{5}{8} =$

$\frac{3}{7} + \frac{3}{14} =$

$\frac{3}{8} + \frac{1}{24} =$

$\frac{2}{9} + \frac{2}{3} =$

$\frac{5}{12} + \frac{1}{4} =$

$\frac{3}{11} + \frac{1}{3} =$

$\frac{1}{8} + \frac{1}{4} =$

$\frac{2}{5} + \frac{1}{2} =$

$\frac{5}{9} + \frac{1}{3} =$

$\frac{5}{6} + \frac{1}{7} =$

$\frac{1}{9} + \frac{1}{3} =$

$\frac{5}{8} + \frac{1}{6} =$

$\frac{11}{16} + \frac{1}{8} =$

$\frac{3}{4} + \frac{1}{7} =$

$\frac{2}{3} + \frac{1}{6} =$

$\frac{33}{80}$	$\frac{6}{40}$	$\frac{6}{13}$	$\frac{33}{40}$
$\frac{6}{14}$	$\frac{3}{21}$	$\frac{9}{14}$	$\frac{6}{21}$
$\frac{4}{24}$	$\frac{5}{12}$	$\frac{4}{32}$	$\frac{10}{24}$
$\frac{4}{27}$	$\frac{4}{9}$	$\frac{8}{9}$	$\frac{4}{12}$
$\frac{8}{12}$	$\frac{6}{16}$	$\frac{4}{6}$	$\frac{2}{3}$
$\frac{3}{33}$	$\frac{4}{14}$	$\frac{20}{33}$	$\frac{3}{14}$
$\frac{2}{8}$	$\frac{3}{8}$	$\frac{1}{12}$	$\frac{2}{12}$
$\frac{9}{10}$	$\frac{3}{7}$	$\frac{4}{5}$	$\frac{3}{10}$
$\frac{6}{9}$	$\frac{8}{9}$	$\frac{16}{18}$	$\frac{6}{12}$
$\frac{41}{42}$	$\frac{6}{13}$	$\frac{6}{7}$	$\frac{5}{42}$
$\frac{2}{9}$	$\frac{4}{9}$	$\frac{2}{3}$	$\frac{1}{12}$
$\frac{6}{14}$	$\frac{6}{8}$	$\frac{19}{24}$	$\frac{6}{48}$
$\frac{12}{24}$	$\frac{12}{16}$	$\frac{11}{16}$	$\frac{13}{16}$
$\frac{4}{11}$	$\frac{3}{28}$	$\frac{25}{28}$	$\frac{3}{11}$
$\frac{4}{6}$	$\frac{3}{18}$	$\frac{3}{9}$	$\frac{5}{6}$

Mars

Jupiter

Saturn

Neptune

Adding fractions with unlike denominators

Dance Party DJ

Name _____ Date _____

Add.
Show your work.
Write the answer in simplest form.

$\dfrac{1}{8} + \dfrac{1}{9} =$	$\dfrac{1}{5}$ $+ \dfrac{2}{3}$ ‾‾‾‾‾	$\dfrac{1}{4} + \dfrac{5}{8} =$	$\dfrac{1}{3}$ $+ \dfrac{3}{8}$ ‾‾‾‾‾
$\dfrac{4}{5}$ $+ \dfrac{1}{9}$ ‾‾‾‾‾	$\dfrac{2}{7} + \dfrac{1}{5} =$	$\dfrac{1}{2}$ $+ \dfrac{5}{11}$ ‾‾‾‾‾	$\dfrac{5}{6} + \dfrac{1}{18} =$
$\dfrac{1}{10}$ $+ \dfrac{3}{4}$ ‾‾‾‾‾	$\dfrac{7}{8} + \dfrac{1}{16} =$	$\dfrac{1}{4} + \dfrac{1}{3} =$	$\dfrac{1}{2}$ $+ \dfrac{1}{3}$ ‾‾‾‾‾
$\dfrac{3}{4} + \dfrac{1}{12} =$	$\dfrac{6}{7}$ $+ \dfrac{1}{8}$ ‾‾‾‾‾	$\dfrac{1}{4}$ $+ \dfrac{5}{16}$ ‾‾‾‾‾	$\dfrac{3}{4} + \dfrac{1}{6} =$

Adding fractions with unlike denominators

Longing for a Goal

Name _____ Date _____

Read.
Show your work on another sheet of paper.
Write the answer in simplest form in the blank.

1. On the Spotstown soccer team, $\frac{1}{4}$ of the players are 9 years old, and $\frac{1}{5}$ of the players are 10 years old. What fraction of the team's players are either 9 or 10 years old? _____ of the team

2. During practice today, $\frac{3}{5}$ of the team practiced dribbling while $\frac{1}{8}$ of the team practiced penalty kicks. What fraction of the team practiced dribbling or penalty kicks? _____ of the team

3. At Wednesday's game, $\frac{1}{7}$ of the team scored a goal. During Thursday's game, $\frac{1}{3}$ of the team scored a goal. What fraction of the team scored a goal during Wednesday's or Thursday's games? _____ of the team

4. During the season, $\frac{1}{10}$ of the games and $\frac{3}{14}$ of the practices were canceled for rain. What fraction of the games and practices were canceled for rain? _____ of the games and practices

5. On the team, $\frac{3}{8}$ of the players can play forward, and $\frac{5}{16}$ of the players can play goalie. What fraction of players can play forward or goalie? _____ of the players

6. The team tied $\frac{1}{6}$ of their games and lost $\frac{1}{18}$ of their games. What fraction of the games did the team lose or tie?
   _____ of the games

Story problems: adding fractions with unlike denominators

"Mane" Attraction

Add.
Show your work.
Write the answer in simplest form.

What's another name for hair?

$2\frac{1}{4}$ $+\ 4\frac{1}{4}$ = A	$3\frac{5}{8}$ $+\ 6\frac{1}{8}$ = R
$5\frac{2}{3}$ $+\ 8\frac{1}{3}$ = R	$1\frac{4}{7}$ $+\ 9\frac{2}{7}$ = T	$7\frac{3}{5}$ $+\ 3\frac{4}{5}$ = E

$8\frac{3}{10}$ $+\ 3\frac{1}{10}$ = E	$2\frac{1}{6}$ $+\ 6\frac{1}{6}$ = O	$4\frac{5}{9}$ $+\ 1\frac{7}{9}$ = R	$9\frac{1}{2}$ $+\ 7\frac{1}{2}$ = N	$6\frac{3}{4}$ $+\ 5\frac{3}{4}$ = A	$1\frac{7}{10}$ $+\ 9\frac{3}{10}$ = G
$2\frac{2}{5}$ $+\ 4\frac{4}{5}$ = P	$3\frac{4}{7}$ $+\ 5\frac{1}{7}$ = E	$7\frac{2}{3}$ $+\ 8\frac{2}{3}$ = T	$2\frac{3}{8}$ $+\ 2\frac{7}{8}$ = A	$4\frac{3}{8}$ $+\ 1\frac{1}{8}$ = C	$6\frac{5}{6}$ $+\ 9\frac{1}{6}$ = I

To answer the question on the mirror, match the letters above to the numbered lines below.

$\overline{}$ $\overline{}$ $\overline{}$ – $\overline{}$ $\overline{}$ – $\overline{}$ $\overline{}$ $\overline{}$ $\qquad$ $\overline{}$ $\overline{}$ $\overline{}$ $\overline{}$ $\overline{}$ $\overline{}$ $\overline{}$ $\overline{}$ $\overline{}$

$8\frac{5}{7}$ $\quad$ $6\frac{1}{2}$ $\quad$ $6\frac{1}{3}$ $\qquad$ $10\frac{6}{7}$ $\quad$ $8\frac{1}{3}$ $\qquad$ $11\frac{2}{5}$ $\quad$ $12\frac{1}{2}$ $\quad$ $9\frac{3}{4}$ $\qquad\qquad$ $5\frac{1}{2}$ $\quad$ $5\frac{1}{4}$ $\quad$ 14 $\quad$ $7\frac{1}{5}$ $\quad$ $11\frac{2}{5}$ $\quad$ $16\frac{1}{3}$ $\quad$ 16 $\quad$ 17 $\quad$ 11

Adding mixed numbers with like denominators

29

Hold On!

Name _____ Date _____

Add.
Show your work on another sheet of paper.
Color if correct.

$1\frac{3}{10} + 4\frac{2}{5} = 5\frac{7}{10}$

$5\frac{1}{4} + 1\frac{1}{3} = 6\frac{7}{12}$

$3\frac{5}{8} + 5\frac{3}{4} = 9\frac{3}{8}$

$2\frac{1}{3} + 6\frac{2}{3} = 9\frac{1}{3}$

$6\frac{3}{10} + 7\frac{7}{10} = 15$

$7\frac{3}{4} + 5\frac{1}{2} = 13\frac{1}{2}$

$4\frac{6}{7} + 6\frac{13}{14} = 11\frac{11}{14}$

$8\frac{2}{3} + 1\frac{5}{6} = 10\frac{1}{2}$

$11\frac{5}{8} + 3\frac{1}{6} = 14\frac{6}{8}$

$5\frac{5}{9} + 8\frac{8}{9} = 15\frac{4}{9}$

$20\frac{4}{7} + 9\frac{2}{7} = 29\frac{6}{7}$

$9\frac{3}{5} + 2\frac{2}{5} = 12$

$15\frac{3}{8} + 2\frac{1}{3} = 15\frac{17}{24}$

$10\frac{7}{9} + 4\frac{1}{3} = 15\frac{1}{9}$

$4\frac{2}{5} + 1\frac{4}{5} = 6\frac{1}{5}$

$12\frac{3}{4} + 5\frac{1}{4} = 18$

Sweet Tooth

Name _____ Date _____

Add.
Show your work.
Write the answer in simplest form.
Color the matching answer.
Some jelly beans will not be colored.

$7 \frac{3}{8}$
$+ 4 \frac{2}{5}$

$4 \frac{3}{7}$
$+ 2 \frac{1}{3}$

$3 \frac{1}{4}$
$+ 8 \frac{3}{4}$

$1 \frac{1}{2}$
$+ 3 \frac{2}{3}$

$5 \frac{7}{8}$
$+ 1 \frac{3}{10}$

$6 \frac{4}{7}$
$+ 7 \frac{6}{7}$

$5 \frac{7}{10}$
$+ 6 \frac{4}{5}$

$5 \frac{3}{4}$
$+ 9 \frac{1}{2}$

$9 \frac{2}{3}$
$+ 2 \frac{2}{3}$

$2 \frac{2}{5}$
$+ 1 \frac{1}{5}$

$8 \frac{1}{2} + 5 \frac{5}{6} =$

$3 \frac{3}{4} + 1 \frac{5}{8} =$

$4 \frac{1}{4} + 1 \frac{2}{3} =$

$9 \frac{3}{5} + 7 \frac{1}{5} =$

$6 \frac{2}{3} + 2 \frac{3}{8} =$

$8 \frac{1}{3} + 1 \frac{2}{9} =$

$3 \frac{3}{5}$

17

12

$14 \frac{2}{6}$

$5 \frac{2}{6}$

$12 \frac{1}{3}$

$5 \frac{3}{8}$

$9 \frac{1}{24}$

$16 \frac{4}{5}$

$14 \frac{3}{7}$

$5 \frac{11}{12}$

$15 \frac{1}{4}$

$9 \frac{5}{9}$

$12 \frac{1}{2}$

$7 \frac{7}{40}$

$5 \frac{1}{6}$

$11 \frac{31}{40}$

$6 \frac{16}{21}$

$14 \frac{1}{3}$

Adding mixed numbers with like and unlike denominators

Bake Sale Goodies

Name _____ Date _____

Read.
Show your work on another sheet of paper.
Write the answer in simplest form in the blank provided.

Follow me to the bake sale!

1.
Becky is making brownies for the bake sale. The recipe calls for $1\frac{1}{2}$ cups of walnuts and $1\frac{1}{4}$ cups of pecans. How many total cups of nuts will Becky need for the cake?

_____ cups

2.
Chris will make his favorite peanut butter cookies. He has already added $2\frac{1}{3}$ cups of flour and $1\frac{1}{2}$ cups of sugar. How much flour and sugar has Chris added all together?

_____ cups

3.
To make his grand- mother's best rolls, Hal needs $2\frac{1}{4}$ teaspoons of dry yeast and $1\frac{3}{4}$ teaspoons of salt. How much salt and yeast does Hal need?

_____ teaspoons

4.
The roll dough has to rise for $2\frac{1}{2}$ hours. After Hal shapes the rolls, they need to rise for $1\frac{1}{2}$ hours more. How many total hours does the roll dough need to rise?

_____ hours

5.
Hal has $3\frac{1}{4}$ dozen rolls for the bake sale. Dan brought $1\frac{5}{8}$ dozen cookies for the sale. How many dozens of treats do Hal and Dan have in all for the bake sale?

_____ dozens

6.
Anna is baking $1\frac{5}{6}$ dozen cupcakes. She is also making $2\frac{1}{2}$ dozen popcorn balls. How many dozens of treats is Anna bringing to the bake sale?

_____ dozens

Subtracting Fractions

Subtracting Fractions

Table of Contents

**Parent Communication
and Student Checkups**

See pages 98–107 for corresponding parent communications
and student checkups (mini tests) for the skills listed above.

Flower Power

Name _____ Date _____

Subtract.
Show your work.
Color the flower with the matching answer.
Some flowers will not be colored.

$\dfrac{7}{11}$ $-\dfrac{3}{11}$

$\dfrac{2}{3}$ $-\dfrac{1}{3}$

$\dfrac{4}{5}$ $-\dfrac{2}{5}$

$\dfrac{8}{17}$ $-\dfrac{4}{17}$

$\dfrac{10}{21}$ $-\dfrac{8}{21}$

$\dfrac{3}{5}$ $-\dfrac{2}{5}$

$\dfrac{7}{9}$ $-\dfrac{5}{9}$

$\dfrac{6}{7}$ $-\dfrac{2}{7}$

$\dfrac{14}{15}$ $-\dfrac{1}{15}$

$\dfrac{17}{19}$ $-\dfrac{5}{19}$

$\dfrac{15}{23}$ $-\dfrac{5}{23}$

$\dfrac{5}{7}$ $-\dfrac{2}{7}$

$\dfrac{8}{9}$ $-\dfrac{4}{9}$

$\dfrac{10}{11}$ $-\dfrac{3}{11}$

$\dfrac{6}{7}$ $-\dfrac{1}{7}$

$\dfrac{13}{15}$ $-\dfrac{11}{15}$

$\dfrac{11}{13}$ $-\dfrac{6}{13}$

$\dfrac{23}{35}$ $-\dfrac{11}{35}$

Wow! That smells good!

Subtracting fractions with like denominators

House-Hunting Hermie

Name _____ Date _____

Subtract.
Show your work on another sheet of paper.
Write the answer in simplest form.
Color if correct.
Connect the colored boxes to show the path to the shell.

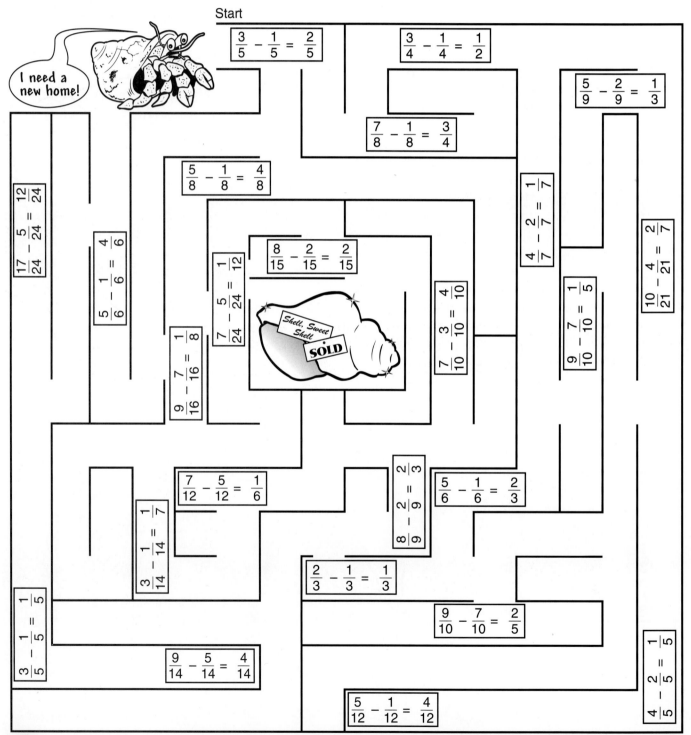

On the Beach

Subtract.
Show your work.
Write the answer in simplest form.
Color by the code.

Color Code

$\frac{1}{2}$ = blue $\frac{1}{5}$ = green

$\frac{1}{3}$ = purple $\frac{1}{6}$ = orange

$\frac{1}{4}$ = brown $\frac{1}{7}$ = yellow

$$\frac{3}{4} - \frac{2}{4}$$

$$\frac{5}{8} - \frac{3}{8}$$

$$\frac{7}{16} - \frac{3}{16} =$$

$$\frac{4}{9} - \frac{1}{9}$$

$$\frac{3}{10} - \frac{1}{10}$$

$$\frac{5}{8} - \frac{1}{8}$$

$$\frac{5}{14} - \frac{3}{14}$$

$$\frac{11}{24} - \frac{7}{24} =$$

$$\frac{11}{24} - \frac{5}{24}$$

$$\frac{7}{12} - \frac{1}{12}$$

$$\frac{4}{5} - \frac{3}{5}$$

$$\frac{2}{3} - \frac{1}{3}$$

$$\frac{3}{8} - \frac{1}{8}$$

$$\frac{7}{24} - \frac{1}{24}$$

$$\frac{11}{32} - \frac{3}{32}$$

$$\frac{7}{8} - \frac{5}{8}$$

$$\frac{9}{16} - \frac{5}{16} =$$

$$\frac{3}{4} - \frac{1}{4}$$

$$\frac{17}{20} - \frac{7}{20}$$

$$\frac{9}{16} - \frac{1}{16}$$

$$\frac{17}{24} - \frac{5}{24}$$

$$\frac{7}{8} - \frac{3}{8}$$

Picture-Perfect

Name _____ Date _____

Read.
Show your work.
Write the answer in simplest form in the blank.

1. Pete had $\frac{3}{4}$ of a tube of blue paint. He used $\frac{1}{4}$ of the paint on a picture. How much paint was left?

   _____ of a tube

2. Polly bought a tube of green paint. She used $\frac{2}{9}$ of it to finish a picture. How much paint did she have left?

   _____ of a tube

3. Paul had a full tube of yellow paint. He had $\frac{1}{10}$ of the tube left when he finished a portrait. How much yellow paint did he use on the portrait?

   _____ of a tube

4. Patty spent $\frac{2}{3}$ of the day painting and spent the rest of the day cleaning. What fraction of the day did she spend cleaning?

   _____ of the day

5. Paco sketched for $\frac{2}{5}$ of the morning and spent the rest of the morning painting. What fraction of the morning did he spend painting?

   _____ of the morning

6. Pearl used $\frac{5}{12}$ of her orange paint on one painting and used the rest of the paint on another painting. How much orange paint did she use on the second painting?

   _____ of the orange paint

Story problems: subtracting fractions with like denominators

Alley-Oop!

Name _____ Date _____

Subtract.
Show your work.
Write the answer in simplest form.

$\dfrac{1}{2}$
$-\dfrac{1}{4}$

$\dfrac{2}{3}$
$-\dfrac{1}{6}$

$\dfrac{4}{7}$
$-\dfrac{1}{14}$

$\dfrac{4}{5}$
$-\dfrac{1}{2}$

$\dfrac{7}{10}$
$-\dfrac{1}{5}$

$\dfrac{4}{5}$
$-\dfrac{3}{10}$

$\dfrac{5}{8}$
$-\dfrac{1}{2}$

$\dfrac{3}{4}$
$-\dfrac{1}{3}$

$\dfrac{5}{9}$
$-\dfrac{1}{3}$

$\dfrac{3}{5}$
$-\dfrac{4}{15}$

$\dfrac{3}{8}$
$-\dfrac{1}{6}$

$\dfrac{2}{5}$
$-\dfrac{1}{4}$

$\dfrac{11}{12}$
$-\dfrac{5}{6}$

$\dfrac{3}{4}$
$-\dfrac{1}{16}$

$\dfrac{7}{8}$
$-\dfrac{1}{2}$

$\dfrac{7}{12}$
$-\dfrac{1}{6}$

Subtracting fractions with unlike denominators

New Moon's Mission

Name _____ Date _____

Subtract.
Show your work.
Write the answer in simplest form.

Why did the moon go to the bank?

$\frac{2}{3} - \frac{1}{5} =$ $\frac{3}{4} - \frac{2}{3} =$

$\frac{5}{8} - \frac{1}{3} =$ $\frac{5}{6} - \frac{5}{12} =$

$\frac{7}{8} - \frac{3}{4} =$ $\frac{4}{9} - \frac{1}{3} =$ $\frac{9}{10} - \frac{4}{5} =$

$\frac{5}{12} - \frac{3}{8} =$ $\frac{3}{5} - \frac{7}{15} =$ $\frac{4}{7} - \frac{1}{3} =$

$\frac{1}{2} - \frac{1}{8} =$ $\frac{4}{5} - \frac{3}{8} =$ $\frac{1}{4} - \frac{1}{6} =$

$\frac{1}{2} - \frac{1}{3} =$ $\frac{6}{7} - \frac{1}{2} =$ $\frac{8}{9} - \frac{2}{3} =$

To answer the riddle, color the letter below that contains each correct answer.

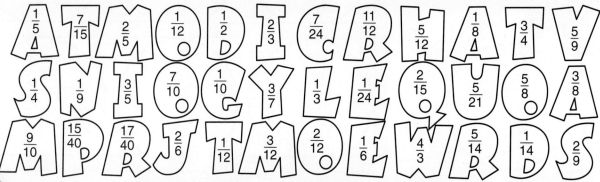

Macaroni and Cheese, Please!

Name _____   Date _____

Subtract.
Show your work on another sheet of paper.
Color if correct.

$$\frac{5}{6} - \frac{1}{3} = \frac{2}{3}$$

$$\begin{array}{r} \frac{2}{3} \\ -\ \frac{1}{4} \\ \hline \frac{5}{12} \end{array}$$

$$\frac{3}{8} - \frac{1}{5} = \frac{7}{40}$$

$$\begin{array}{r} \frac{7}{8} \\ -\ \frac{1}{6} \\ \hline \frac{2}{3} \end{array}$$

$$\begin{array}{r} \frac{4}{5} \\ -\ \frac{1}{2} \\ \hline \frac{3}{10} \end{array}$$

$$\begin{array}{r} \frac{4}{9} \\ -\ \frac{1}{3} \\ \hline \frac{1}{3} \end{array}$$

$$\frac{3}{7} - \frac{1}{3} = \frac{2}{21}$$

$$\frac{5}{6} - \frac{3}{4} = \frac{1}{12}$$

$$\begin{array}{r} \frac{1}{2} \\ -\ \frac{1}{4} \\ \hline \frac{2}{4} \end{array}$$

$$\frac{11}{12} - \frac{2}{3} = \frac{1}{12}$$

$$\begin{array}{r} \frac{1}{2} \\ -\ \frac{5}{12} \\ \hline \frac{1}{12} \end{array}$$

$$\begin{array}{r} \frac{8}{9} \\ -\ \frac{2}{3} \\ \hline \frac{2}{3} \end{array}$$

$$\begin{array}{r} \frac{3}{4} \\ -\ \frac{3}{8} \\ \hline \frac{3}{8} \end{array}$$

$$\frac{1}{2} - \frac{3}{10} = \frac{1}{5}$$

$$\begin{array}{r} \frac{2}{5} \\ -\ \frac{1}{10} \\ \hline \frac{3}{10} \end{array}$$

$$\frac{7}{8} - \frac{3}{4} = \frac{1}{8}$$

$$\begin{array}{r} \frac{5}{8} \\ -\ \frac{1}{3} \\ \hline \frac{7}{18} \end{array}$$

$$\frac{5}{7} - \frac{1}{3} = \frac{8}{21}$$

$$\begin{array}{r} \frac{7}{12} \\ -\ \frac{1}{8} \\ \hline \frac{10}{24} \end{array}$$

$$\frac{9}{10} - \frac{3}{5} = \frac{3}{10}$$

"Stud-ant" Field Trip

Name _____ Date _____

Read.
Show your work on another sheet of paper.
Write each answer in simplest form in the blank provided.

1. For their spring field trip, the students at "Alex-ant-er" Academy hiked to Ant Hill. Of all the students, $\frac{2}{3}$ brought bag lunches and $\frac{2}{5}$ bought their lunches. How many more students brought lunches than bought lunches?

   _____ of the students

2. For the hike, $\frac{5}{6}$ of the students brought water bottles, while $\frac{1}{8}$ of the students brought sports drinks. How many more students brought water bottles than sports drinks?

   _____ of the students

3. Before lunch, the class hiked $\frac{4}{5}$ of a mile toward Ant Hill. After lunch, the class hiked $\frac{3}{4}$ of a mile toward Ant Hill. How much farther did the class hike in the morning than in the afternoon?

   _____ of a mile

4. Everyone in the class wore a hat. Baseball caps made up $\frac{5}{8}$ of the hats, while $\frac{1}{4}$ of the hats were floppy hats. How many more hats were baseball caps than floppy hats?

   _____ of the hats

5. After both hikes, $\frac{3}{5}$ of the students had snacks and $\frac{1}{3}$ had drinks. How many more students had snacks than drinks?

   _____ of the students

6. On the bus ride home, $\frac{1}{2}$ of the students fell asleep, and $\frac{2}{5}$ of the students talked the whole way. How many more students fell asleep than talked?

   _____ of the students

It's in the Mail!

Name _____ Date _____

Subtract.
Show your work.
Write the answer in simplest form.
Cross off the answer on the mailbox.
Some numbers will not be crossed off.

U.S. MAIL

$2\frac{1}{3}$	$5\frac{1}{3}$
$2\frac{1}{3}$	$2\frac{2}{3}$
$1\frac{1}{8}$	$1\frac{1}{16}$
$1\frac{1}{5}$	$3\frac{3}{5}$
$1\frac{1}{6}$	$11\frac{1}{2}$
$7\frac{2}{9}$	$1\frac{1}{7}$
$1\frac{2}{3}$	$6\frac{3}{5}$
$2\frac{3}{10}$	$6\frac{6}{10}$
$3\frac{1}{4}$	$3\frac{1}{3}$

$2\frac{4}{7}$
$- 1\frac{3}{7}$

$5\frac{3}{8}$
$- 2\frac{1}{8}$

$4\frac{5}{6}$
$- 2\frac{1}{6}$

$3\frac{2}{3}$
$- 1\frac{1}{3}$

$6\frac{2}{3}$
$- 4\frac{1}{3}$

$9\frac{7}{10}$
$- 3\frac{1}{10}$

$7\frac{8}{9}$
$- 4\frac{5}{9}$

$12\frac{3}{4}$
$- 1\frac{1}{4}$

$9\frac{3}{16}$
$- 8\frac{1}{16}$

$5\frac{7}{12}$
$- 4\frac{5}{12}$

$2\frac{7}{9}$
$- 1\frac{1}{9}$

$3\frac{3}{5}$
$- 2\frac{2}{5}$

$10\frac{5}{18}$
$- 3\frac{1}{18}$

$8\frac{13}{20}$
$- 6\frac{7}{20}$

$9\frac{4}{5}$
$- 6\frac{1}{5}$

$7\frac{4}{9}$
$- 2\frac{1}{9}$

Who's the Tallest?

Name _____ Date _____

Subtract.
Show your work on another sheet of paper.
Write the answer in simplest form.
Color to show the path to match
   the tallest animal's head
   and feet.

Problem	elephant	camel	llama	giraffe
$12\frac{3}{4} - 2\frac{1}{4} =$	$14\frac{2}{4}$	$10\frac{1}{2}$	$11\frac{1}{2}$	$10\frac{2}{4}$
$7\frac{4}{9} - 3\frac{2}{9} =$	$4\frac{2}{9}$	$4\frac{2}{3}$	$4\frac{1}{9}$	$3\frac{2}{9}$
$11\frac{7}{12} - 4\frac{1}{12} =$	$7\frac{1}{2}$	$8\frac{1}{2}$	$7\frac{5}{12}$	$7\frac{6}{12}$
$17\frac{3}{8} - 6\frac{1}{8} =$	$7\frac{1}{4}$	$11\frac{1}{4}$	$11\frac{2}{8}$	$23\frac{1}{2}$
$5\frac{7}{15} - 3\frac{2}{15} =$	$2\frac{5}{15}$	$2\frac{3}{5}$	$2\frac{1}{3}$	$3\frac{1}{5}$
$9\frac{7}{10} - 1\frac{1}{10} =$	$8\frac{6}{10}$	$10\frac{1}{2}$	$8\frac{3}{5}$	$10\frac{3}{5}$
$12\frac{7}{9} - 5\frac{1}{9} =$	$7\frac{6}{9}$	$6\frac{2}{3}$	$8\frac{5}{9}$	$7\frac{2}{3}$
$6\frac{4}{7} - 3\frac{2}{7} =$	$9\frac{2}{7}$	$3\frac{1}{7}$	$3\frac{2}{7}$	$18\frac{2}{7}$
$15\frac{5}{6} - 14\frac{1}{6} =$	$29\frac{4}{6}$	$1\frac{2}{3}$	$9\frac{2}{3}$	$1\frac{4}{6}$
$11\frac{11}{12} - 4\frac{5}{12} =$	$15\frac{1}{2}$	$7\frac{1}{2}$	$6\frac{6}{12}$	$7\frac{6}{12}$
$8\frac{9}{14} - 3\frac{1}{14} =$	$5\frac{4}{7}$	$11\frac{4}{7}$	$8\frac{8}{14}$	$8\frac{1}{2}$
$11\frac{2}{9} - 4\frac{1}{9} =$	$6\frac{1}{9}$	$7\frac{1}{9}$	$15\frac{1}{9}$	$7\frac{3}{9}$
$5\frac{17}{20} - 3\frac{13}{20} =$	$2\frac{4}{20}$	$2\frac{6}{20}$	$2\frac{1}{5}$	$2\frac{1}{2}$
$17\frac{7}{8} - 12\frac{5}{8} =$	$29\frac{1}{4}$	$5\frac{1}{4}$	$5\frac{2}{5}$	$5\frac{2}{8}$
$9\frac{6}{11} - 4\frac{2}{11} =$	$13\frac{8}{11}$	$5\frac{5}{11}$	$5\frac{4}{11}$	$5\frac{8}{11}$
$3\frac{3}{4} - 1\frac{1}{4} =$	$2\frac{2}{4}$	$2\frac{1}{8}$	$2\frac{1}{2}$	$2\frac{2}{8}$
$8\frac{9}{12} - 4\frac{1}{12} =$	$4\frac{8}{12}$	$4\frac{1}{2}$	$4\frac{5}{6}$	$4\frac{2}{3}$

elephant   camel   llama   giraffe

Subtracting mixed numbers with like denominators

Hen Humor

Name _____   Date _____

Subtract.
Show your work.
Write each answer in simplest form.

What's so funny?

(H) $19\frac{3}{4}$
     $- 7\frac{1}{4}$

(L) $15\frac{7}{8}$
     $- 9\frac{5}{8}$

(O) $43\frac{5}{6}$
     $- 27\frac{1}{6}$

(Y) $4\frac{6}{7}$
     $- 1\frac{3}{7}$

(O) $17\frac{4}{5}$
     $- 9\frac{2}{5}$

(M) $54\frac{9}{10}$
     $- 37\frac{7}{10}$

(B) $32\frac{6}{11}$
     $- 19\frac{4}{11}$

(I) $12\frac{3}{8}$
     $- 9\frac{1}{8}$

(S) $62\frac{4}{9}$
     $- 57\frac{1}{9}$

(T) $26\frac{7}{10}$
     $- 17\frac{1}{10}$

(N) $37\frac{5}{12}$
     $- 18\frac{1}{12}$

(W) $46\frac{7}{11}$
     $- 42\frac{2}{11}$

(A) $63\frac{19}{20}$
     $- 31\frac{11}{20}$

(T) $18\frac{2}{5}$
     $- 16\frac{1}{5}$

(O) $59\frac{9}{14} - 32\frac{5}{14} =$

(A) $96\frac{6}{11} - 74\frac{5}{11} =$

(L) $21\frac{7}{9} - 15\frac{2}{9} =$

(F) $36\frac{9}{10} - 24\frac{3}{10} =$

(L) $45\frac{11}{16} - 38\frac{3}{16} =$

Why aren't chickens good at baseball?
To solve the riddle, match the letters above to the numbered lines below.

They ____ ____ ____   ____ ____ ____   ____ ____ ____ ____
     $12\frac{1}{2}$ $3\frac{1}{4}$ $2\frac{1}{5}$ $9\frac{3}{5}$ $16\frac{2}{3}$ $27\frac{2}{7}$ $17\frac{1}{5}$ $32\frac{2}{5}$ $19\frac{1}{3}$ $3\frac{3}{7}$

     " ____ ____ ____ ____ "   ____ ____ ____ ____ ____ !
       $12\frac{3}{5}$ $8\frac{2}{5}$ $4\frac{5}{11}$ $7\frac{1}{2}$ $13\frac{2}{11}$ $22\frac{1}{11}$ $6\frac{5}{9}$ $6\frac{1}{4}$ $5\frac{1}{3}$

Cooking Class

Name _____ Date _____

Read.
Show your work on another sheet of paper.
Write each answer in simplest form in the blank.

1. Carrie is mixing batter to make fish-shaped pancakes. Her measuring cup has $3\frac{2}{3}$ cups of milk in it. If she pours $2\frac{1}{3}$ cups into the batter, how much milk will be left in the measuring cup? _____ cups

2. Carlos is making catnip cookies. The recipe calls for $2\frac{3}{8}$ teaspoons of catnip. He has already added $1\frac{1}{8}$ teaspoons. How many more teaspoons of catnip does he need to add? _____ teaspoons

3. Candie is making mouse-flavored meatloaf. It must cook for $2\frac{3}{4}$ hours. If it has already cooked for $1\frac{1}{4}$ hours, how much longer should it cook? _____ hours

4. Connor is making tuna casserole. The recipe calls for $7\frac{9}{10}$ ounces of tuna and $3\frac{1}{10}$ ounces of cheese. How many more ounces of tuna than cheese does Connor need? _____ ounces

5. Cara is decorating a mouse-shaped birthday cake. She needs $2\frac{1}{6}$ cups of sugar for the icing. She added $3\frac{5}{6}$ cups by mistake. How much extra sugar did Cara add? _____ cups

6. Cal is making a shopping list for next week's cooking class. He needs to buy $10\frac{3}{5}$ pounds of flour and $4\frac{1}{5}$ pounds of sugar. How many more pounds of flour than sugar does Cal need to buy? _____ pounds

©The Education Center, Inc. • *Target Math Success* • TEC60833 • Key p. 130

Story problems: subtracting mixed numbers with like denominators

Road Hunting

Name _____ Date _____

Subtract.
Show your work on another sheet of paper.
Write each answer in simplest form.

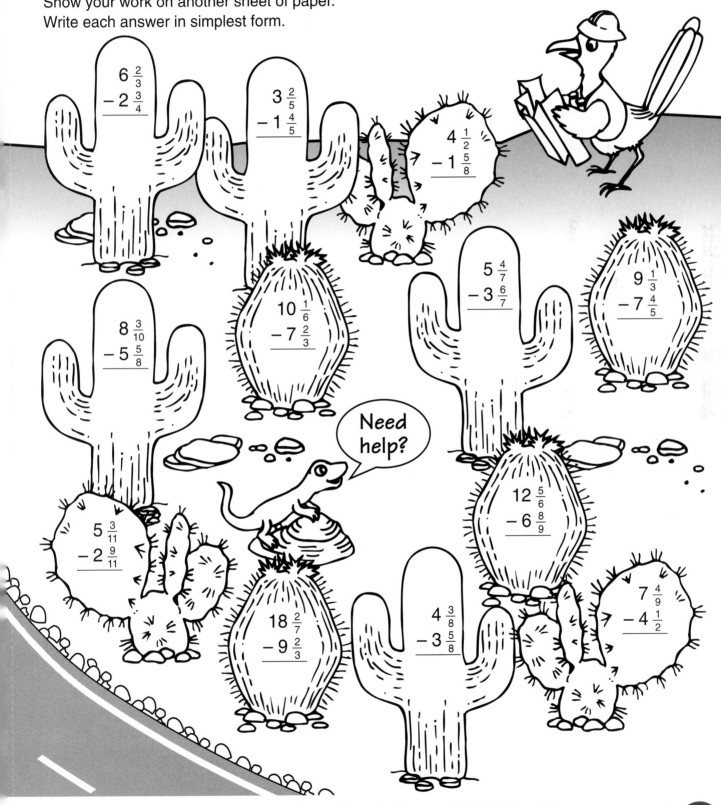

$6\frac{2}{3}$
$-2\frac{3}{4}$

$3\frac{2}{5}$
$-1\frac{4}{5}$

$4\frac{1}{2}$
$-1\frac{5}{8}$

$8\frac{3}{10}$
$-5\frac{5}{8}$

$10\frac{1}{6}$
$-7\frac{2}{3}$

$5\frac{4}{7}$
$-3\frac{6}{7}$

$9\frac{1}{3}$
$-7\frac{4}{5}$

Need help?

$5\frac{3}{11}$
$-2\frac{9}{11}$

$12\frac{5}{6}$
$-6\frac{8}{9}$

$18\frac{2}{7}$
$-9\frac{2}{3}$

$4\frac{3}{8}$
$-3\frac{5}{8}$

$7\frac{4}{9}$
$-4\frac{1}{2}$

Subtracting mixed numbers with like and unlike denominators with regrouping

Around We Go!

Subtract.
Show your work on another sheet of paper.
Write each answer in simplest form.
Color the matching answers.
One number will not be colored.

$1\frac{2}{3}$

$5\frac{19}{21}$

$\frac{13}{24}$

$1\frac{17}{24}$

$1\frac{1}{2}$

$5\frac{3}{4}$

$3\frac{4}{5}$

$4\frac{1}{3}$

$3\frac{11}{12}$

$3\frac{1}{2}$

$5\frac{9}{10}$

$7\frac{2}{3}$

$\frac{13}{14}$

$3\frac{5}{8}$

$1\frac{1}{8}$

$9\frac{1}{3} - 1\frac{2}{3} =$ ☐

$7\frac{1}{6} - 3\frac{1}{4} =$ ☐

$13\frac{2}{9} - 8\frac{8}{9} =$ ☐

$6\frac{1}{5} - 2\frac{7}{10} =$ ☐

$7\frac{4}{9} - 5\frac{7}{9} =$ ☐

$3\frac{3}{8} - 2\frac{5}{6} =$ ☐

$5\frac{1}{2} - 1\frac{7}{8} =$ ☐

$4\frac{3}{7} - 3\frac{1}{2} =$ ☐

$12\frac{3}{8} - 6\frac{5}{8} =$ ☐

$9\frac{4}{7} - 3\frac{2}{3} =$ ☐

$6\frac{1}{4} - 4\frac{3}{4} =$ ☐

$2\frac{7}{8} - 1\frac{3}{4} =$ ☐

$8\frac{3}{5} - 4\frac{4}{5} =$ ☐

$11\frac{1}{3} - 9\frac{5}{8} =$ ☐

Subtracting mixed numbers with like and unlike denominators with regrouping

If Wishes Were Fishes...

Name _____ Date _____

Subtract.
Show your work on another sheet of paper.
Write each answer in simplest form.
Color by the code.

Color Code
less than 1 = brown
between 1 and 4 = gray
greater than 4 = blue

$4\frac{5}{12}$
$-3\frac{1}{2}$

$2\frac{1}{3}$
$-1\frac{2}{3}$

$2\frac{2}{7} - 1\frac{1}{2} =$

$2\frac{5}{8} - 1\frac{3}{4} =$

$7\frac{3}{10} - 6\frac{9}{10} =$

$15\frac{2}{3} - 14\frac{7}{8} =$

$5\frac{1}{6}$
$-3\frac{2}{5}$

$10\frac{1}{2}$
$-6\frac{2}{3}$

$8\frac{3}{8}$
$-2\frac{5}{8}$

$9\frac{2}{5}$
$-6\frac{4}{5}$

$11\frac{3}{5}$
$-8\frac{9}{10}$

$8\frac{2}{3}$
$-1\frac{6}{7}$

$7\frac{3}{4}$
$-3\frac{5}{6}$

$13\frac{1}{4}$
$-11\frac{5}{7}$

$12\frac{1}{6} - 4\frac{1}{9} =$

$15\frac{1}{3} - 5\frac{8}{9} =$

Subtracting mixed numbers with like and unlike denominators with regrouping

Treetop Construction

Name _____   Date _____

Read.
Solve each problem on another sheet of paper.
Write each answer in simplest form in the blank provided.

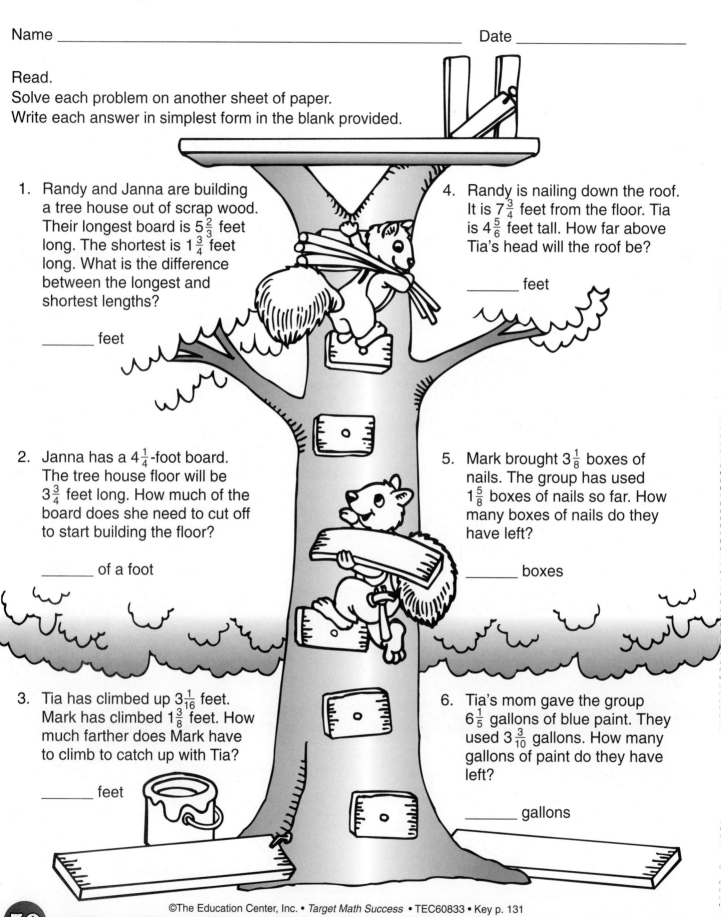

1. Randy and Janna are building a tree house out of scrap wood. Their longest board is $5\frac{2}{3}$ feet long. The shortest is $1\frac{3}{4}$ feet long. What is the difference between the longest and shortest lengths?

   _____ feet

2. Janna has a $4\frac{1}{4}$-foot board. The tree house floor will be $3\frac{3}{4}$ feet long. How much of the board does she need to cut off to start building the floor?

   _____ of a foot

3. Tia has climbed up $3\frac{1}{16}$ feet. Mark has climbed $1\frac{3}{8}$ feet. How much farther does Mark have to climb to catch up with Tia?

   _____ feet

4. Randy is nailing down the roof. It is $7\frac{3}{4}$ feet from the floor. Tia is $4\frac{5}{6}$ feet tall. How far above Tia's head will the roof be?

   _____ feet

5. Mark brought $3\frac{1}{8}$ boxes of nails. The group has used $1\frac{5}{8}$ boxes of nails so far. How many boxes of nails do they have left?

   _____ boxes

6. Tia's mom gave the group $6\frac{1}{5}$ gallons of blue paint. They used $3\frac{3}{10}$ gallons. How many gallons of paint do they have left?

   _____ gallons

©The Education Center, Inc. • *Target Math Success* • TEC60833 • Key p. 131
Story problems: subtracting mixed numbers with like and unlike denominators with regrouping

Crack a Book!

Name _____ Date _____

Subtract.
Show your work.
Write the answer in simplest form.

This book
is great!

$15 - \frac{6}{7}$

$8 - \frac{2}{9}$

$2 - \frac{5}{6}$

$36 - \frac{3}{8}$

I know. I
loved it!

$75 - \frac{3}{4}$

$26 - \frac{1}{8}$

$52 - \frac{4}{7}$

$12 - \frac{1}{5}$

Who's the
author?

$1 - \frac{3}{5}$

$7 - \frac{6}{17}$

$46 - \frac{12}{13}$

$39 - \frac{2}{3}$

$10 - \frac{7}{11}$

$62 - \frac{7}{8}$

On Your Mark, Get Set, Go!

Name _____   Date _____

Subtract.
Show your work.
Write the answer in simplest form.
Color the boxes with answers greater than 20 to show the path to the trophy.

$30 - \frac{3}{5} =$	$28 - \frac{4}{9} =$	$2 - \frac{3}{8} =$

Start

$9 - \frac{7}{18} =$	$26 - \frac{3}{7} =$	$54 - \frac{2}{9} =$	$21 - \frac{2}{3} =$	$1 - \frac{1}{10} =$
$21 - \frac{14}{15} =$	$64 - \frac{2}{9} =$	$3 - \frac{1}{12} =$	$16 - \frac{1}{2} =$	$9 - \frac{3}{4} =$
$37 - \frac{1}{2} =$	$13 - \frac{5}{7} =$	$7 - \frac{1}{6} =$	$2 - \frac{19}{20} =$	$14 - \frac{2}{5} =$
$50 - \frac{1}{11} =$	$74 - \frac{7}{9} =$	$22 - \frac{1}{4} =$	Finish line	

Subtracting fractions from whole numbers

Billionaire Baker

Name _____ Date _____

Subtract.
Show your work.
Write the answer in simplest form.
To solve the riddle, match the letters to the numbered
  lines below.

A $\quad 4$
   $- \frac{1}{2}$

L $\quad 12$
   $- \frac{5}{8}$

O $\quad 17$
   $- \frac{5}{6}$

T $\quad 23$
   $- \frac{7}{12}$

E $\quad 16$
   $- \frac{7}{8}$

F $\quad 10$
   $- \frac{1}{4}$

O $\quad 5$
   $- \frac{9}{10}$

G $\quad 63$
   $- \frac{5}{7}$

A $\quad 6$
   $- \frac{2}{13}$

O $3 - \frac{1}{9} =$

D $28 - \frac{1}{6} =$

M $11 - \frac{3}{16} =$

U $14 - \frac{2}{3} =$

H $74 - \frac{11}{20} =$

D $8 - \frac{5}{18} =$

How did the baker get so rich?

He ___ ___ ___ ___   ___   ___ ___ ___
   $10\frac{13}{16}$ $3\frac{1}{2}$ $27\frac{5}{6}$ $15\frac{1}{8}$ $5\frac{11}{13}$ $11\frac{3}{8}$ $4\frac{1}{10}$ $22\frac{5}{12}$

   ___ ___   ___ ___ ___ ___ ___ !
   $2\frac{8}{9}$ $9\frac{3}{4}$ $7\frac{13}{18}$ $16\frac{1}{6}$ $13\frac{1}{3}$ $62\frac{2}{7}$ $73\frac{9}{20}$

Subtracting fractions from whole numbers

Polly's Pets

Name _____ Date _____

Read.
Solve each problem on
   another sheet of paper.
Write the answer in simplest
   form in the blank.

---

1. Polly prepared an aquarium for her new fish. She had 2 pounds of rocks and used $\frac{7}{8}$ of a pound in the aquarium. How many pounds of rocks were left?

   _____ pounds

2. Peter, Polly's brother, filled the bird's water bottle. He started with an 8-ounce cup of water and poured $\frac{3}{4}$ of an ounce in the bottle. How many ounces were left in the cup?

   _____ ounces

3. Polly had an 18-pound bag of dog food. She poured $\frac{3}{5}$ of a pound into her dog's bowl. How many pounds of dog food were left in the bag?

   _____ pounds

4. Polly's cat had 6 ounces of cat food in its dish. One-seventh of an ounce was left after the cat ate. How many ounces of cat food did the cat eat?

   _____ ounces

5. Peter cleaned the hamster cage and put down $\frac{9}{10}$ of a pound of wood chips. If he started with a 10-pound bag of wood chips, how many pounds of wood chips were left in the bag?

   _____ pounds

6. Polly fed her turtle last. She had 1 pound of food and gave the turtle $\frac{5}{9}$ of a pound. How many pounds of food were left?

   _____ pounds

Story problems: subtracting fractions from whole numbers

Takin' a Break

Name _____ Date _____

Subtract.
Show your work.
Write each answer in simplest form.
Color the matching answer on the wheel.
Some wheels will not be colored.

Barkersville
Rest Stop

$$6\tfrac{1}{5} - \tfrac{1}{3}$$

$$7\tfrac{1}{3} - \tfrac{5}{6}$$

$$2\tfrac{3}{10} - \tfrac{1}{2}$$

$$3\tfrac{4}{5} - \tfrac{6}{7}$$

$3\tfrac{13}{21}$ $1\tfrac{4}{5}$ $2\tfrac{33}{35}$ $6\tfrac{1}{2}$ $5\tfrac{13}{15}$

$$5\tfrac{1}{3} - \tfrac{5}{8}$$

$$8\tfrac{3}{5} - \tfrac{3}{4}$$

$$1\tfrac{1}{4} - \tfrac{7}{9}$$

$$9\tfrac{3}{8} - \tfrac{4}{5}$$

$\tfrac{17}{36}$ $4\tfrac{17}{24}$ $8\tfrac{23}{40}$ $7\tfrac{17}{20}$ $11\tfrac{5}{8}$

$$10\tfrac{1}{8} - \tfrac{2}{5}$$

$$12\tfrac{1}{6} - \tfrac{8}{9}$$

$$20\tfrac{2}{9} - \tfrac{5}{7}$$

$$17\tfrac{2}{3} - \tfrac{9}{10}$$

 $16\tfrac{23}{30}$ $11\tfrac{5}{18}$  $19\tfrac{32}{63}$ $9\tfrac{29}{40}$

Subtracting fractions from mixed numbers

Just Beachy!

Name _____   Date _____

Subtract.
Show your work on another sheet of paper.
Write each answer in simplest form.
Color by the code.

$3\frac{2}{5} - \frac{7}{10} =$ _____

$7\frac{1}{3} - \frac{4}{21} =$ _____

$10\frac{1}{4} - \frac{5}{12} =$ _____

$4\frac{1}{2} - \frac{5}{6} =$ _____

$5\frac{1}{8} - \frac{2}{3} =$ _____

$15\frac{1}{6} - \frac{5}{12} =$ _____

$12\frac{3}{5} - \frac{7}{8} =$ _____

$11\frac{5}{8} - \frac{3}{4} =$ _____

$1\frac{1}{5} - \frac{8}{15} =$ _____

$2\frac{2}{7} - \frac{9}{14} =$ _____

$1\frac{3}{8} - \frac{5}{16} =$ _____

$3\frac{1}{6} - \frac{5}{18} =$ _____

$4\frac{5}{9} - \frac{13}{18} =$ _____

$5\frac{4}{9} - \frac{1}{2} =$ _____

$9\frac{2}{3} - \frac{11}{12} =$ _____

$8\frac{1}{2} - \frac{4}{5} =$ _____

Subtracting fractions from mixed numbers

Craggy-Croc Skin Solution

Name _____ Date _____

Subtract.
Show your work on another sheet of paper.
Color if correct.
Connect the colored boxes to show the path to the jar.

Start

$15\frac{1}{4} - \frac{3}{7} = 15\frac{24}{28}$

$3\frac{3}{4} - \frac{7}{8} = 2\frac{7}{8}$

$1\frac{2}{5} - \frac{5}{9} = \frac{4}{9}$

$14\frac{2}{7} - \frac{1}{3} = 14\frac{13}{14}$

$\begin{array}{r} 6\frac{1}{9} \\ -\ \frac{1}{3} \\ \hline 6\frac{7}{9} \end{array}$

$20\frac{1}{8} - \frac{5}{6} = 19\frac{7}{24}$

$\begin{array}{r} 11\frac{2}{3} \\ -\ \frac{5}{6} \\ \hline 10\frac{5}{6} \end{array}$

$\begin{array}{r} 8\frac{1}{9} \\ -\ \frac{1}{3} \\ \hline 8\frac{7}{9} \end{array}$

$\begin{array}{r} 4\frac{1}{2} \\ -\ \frac{5}{8} \\ \hline 3\frac{5}{8} \end{array}$

Softer Skin in 7 Days!
(Guaranteed)
Skin Cream

$18\frac{3}{7} - \frac{1}{2} = 17\frac{13}{14}$

$9\frac{1}{4} - \frac{4}{9} = 9\frac{29}{36}$

$16\frac{1}{3}$
$-\ \frac{5}{7}$
$\overline{15\frac{13}{21}}$

$\begin{array}{r} 1\frac{3}{4} \\ -\ \frac{4}{5} \\ \hline \frac{19}{20} \end{array}$

$\begin{array}{r} 2\frac{1}{5} \\ -\ \frac{2}{3} \\ \hline 1\frac{8}{16} \end{array}$

$5\frac{3}{5} - \frac{14}{15} = 4\frac{2}{3}$

$13\frac{1}{6} - \frac{7}{9} = 12\frac{7}{9}$

Subtracting fractions from mixed numbers

Water Strider on Skis!

Name _____ Date _____

Read.
Solve each problem on another sheet of paper.
Write each answer in simplest form in the blank provided.

1. Wally loves to water-ski! He has been skiing for $3\frac{1}{2}$ months. He couldn't ski for $\frac{3}{4}$ of one month because his boat had a leak. For how many months has Wally actually skied?

    _____ months

2. Wally is learning to jump off a ramp. The pond record is $7\frac{1}{2}$ inches. Wally's best jump is $\frac{5}{8}$ of an inch shorter than the record. How far is Wally's best jump?

    _____ inches

3. Wally's favorite pair of skis are $1\frac{1}{4}$ inches long. His trick skis are $\frac{3}{8}$ of an inch shorter. How long are Wally's trick skis?

    _____ of an inch

4. Wally's best time skiing around the slalom course is $8\frac{1}{3}$ seconds. His second-best time is $\frac{4}{9}$ of a second slower. What is Wally's second-best time skiing the slalom?

    _____ seconds

5. Wally just shortened his towline by $\frac{9}{10}$ of a centimeter. If the towline was $9\frac{2}{5}$ centimeters long to begin with, how long is his towline now?

    _____ centimeters

6. Wally skies best when his boat is going $9\frac{1}{6}$ miles per hour. When the water surface gets rough, he likes to go $\frac{3}{5}$ of a mile per hour slower. How fast does Wally like to go when the water surface is rough?

    _____ miles per hour

Multiplying Fractions

Multiplying Fractions

Table of Contents

Parent Communication and Student Checkups

See pages 108–115 for corresponding parent communications and student checkups (mini tests) for the skills listed above.

"Haaave" You Heard?

Name _____ Date _____

Multiply.
Show your work.
Write each answer in simplest form.
To solve the riddle, match the letters to the numbered lines below.
Some letters will not be used.

B
$\frac{2}{3}$ x $\frac{3}{12}$ =

T
$\frac{1}{2}$ x $\frac{1}{2}$ =

A
$\frac{1}{8}$ x $\frac{3}{4}$ =

G
$\frac{2}{5}$ x $\frac{3}{7}$ =

Q
$\frac{7}{9}$ x $\frac{5}{6}$ =

E
$\frac{3}{5}$ x $\frac{5}{8}$ =

L
$\frac{1}{6}$ x $\frac{1}{3}$ =

S
$\frac{1}{4}$ x $\frac{2}{7}$ =

Y
$\frac{1}{?}$ x $\frac{4}{8}$ =

O
$\frac{1}{6}$ x $\frac{7}{8}$ =

D
$\frac{2}{3}$ x $\frac{1}{6}$ =

P
$\frac{3}{7}$ x $\frac{5}{8}$ =

R
$\frac{2}{15}$ x $\frac{3}{4}$ =

N
$\frac{2}{9}$ x $\frac{3}{9}$ =

H
$\frac{7}{10}$ x $\frac{2}{3}$ =

Why did the farmer's wife think no one listened to her?

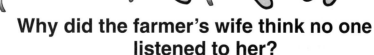

$\frac{7}{48}$ $\frac{2}{27}$ $\frac{1}{18}$ $\frac{1}{12}$ $\frac{1}{4}$ $\frac{7}{15}$ $\frac{3}{8}$ $\frac{1}{14}$ $\frac{7}{15}$ $\frac{3}{8}$ $\frac{3}{8}$ $\frac{15}{56}$

"   "

$\frac{7}{15}$ $\frac{3}{8}$ $\frac{1}{10}$ $\frac{1}{9}$ $\frac{7}{15}$ $\frac{3}{8}$ $\frac{1}{10}$.

©The Education Center, Inc. • *Target Math Success* • TEC60833 • Key p. 132

A "Purr-fect" Princess

Name _____   Date _____

Multiply.
Show your work.
Write each answer in simplest form.
Cross off the answer on the towers.
Some answers will not be crossed off.

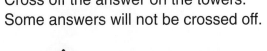

Left tower
$\dfrac{6}{35}$
$\dfrac{2}{5}$
$\dfrac{3}{32}$
$\dfrac{4}{5}$
$\dfrac{1}{6}$
$\dfrac{7}{16}$
$\dfrac{1}{2}$
$\dfrac{10}{63}$
$\dfrac{1}{20}$
$\dfrac{2}{21}$

$\dfrac{1}{3} \times \dfrac{5}{6} =$ $\dfrac{4}{5} \times \dfrac{1}{2} =$ $\dfrac{1}{3} \times \dfrac{1}{2} =$

$\dfrac{5}{6} \times \dfrac{3}{4} =$ $\dfrac{1}{4} \times \dfrac{1}{5} =$ $\dfrac{2}{3} \times \dfrac{1}{4} =$

$\dfrac{3}{5} \times \dfrac{3}{5} =$ $\dfrac{1}{2} \times \dfrac{7}{8} =$ $\dfrac{1}{4} \times \dfrac{3}{8} =$

$\dfrac{2}{3} \times \dfrac{5}{8} =$ $\dfrac{2}{5} \times \dfrac{3}{7} =$ $\dfrac{5}{9} \times \dfrac{2}{7} =$

$\dfrac{1}{4} \times \dfrac{3}{5} =$ $\dfrac{3}{4} \times \dfrac{3}{5} =$ $\dfrac{2}{3} \times \dfrac{6}{8} =$

$\dfrac{5}{9} \times \dfrac{3}{10} =$ $\dfrac{7}{8} \times \dfrac{3}{4} =$ $\dfrac{3}{7} \times \dfrac{2}{9} =$

Right tower
$\dfrac{5}{8}$
$\dfrac{3}{20}$
$\dfrac{1}{6}$
$\dfrac{5}{18}$
$\dfrac{5}{12}$
$\dfrac{9}{20}$
$\dfrac{9}{25}$
$\dfrac{6}{20}$
$\dfrac{1}{6}$
$\dfrac{21}{32}$

Multiplying fractions by fractions

Love Bugs

Name _____ Date _____

Multiply.
Show your work on another sheet of paper.
Write each answer in simplest form.
Color if correct.

$\frac{1}{3} \times \frac{2}{3} = \frac{2}{9}$

$\frac{4}{9} \times \frac{3}{5} = \frac{12}{45}$

$\frac{3}{4} \times \frac{8}{9} = \frac{2}{3}$

$\frac{1}{8} \times \frac{4}{5} = \frac{1}{10}$

$\frac{4}{7} \times \frac{1}{5} = \frac{4}{35}$

$\frac{1}{4} \times \frac{3}{4} = \frac{3}{8}$

$\frac{1}{9} \times \frac{3}{5} = \frac{1}{15}$

$\frac{9}{10} \times \frac{2}{3} = \frac{9}{15}$

$\frac{1}{5} \times \frac{1}{2} = \frac{1}{10}$

$\frac{5}{6} \times \frac{2}{3} = \frac{5}{9}$

$\frac{4}{7} \times \frac{3}{5} = \frac{7}{12}$

$\frac{2}{5} \times \frac{1}{4} = \frac{1}{10}$

$\frac{7}{12} \times \frac{2}{3} = \frac{7}{15}$

$\frac{10}{11} \times \frac{4}{5} = \frac{5}{11}$

$\frac{3}{7} \times \frac{5}{6} = \frac{5}{14}$

$\frac{2}{3} \times \frac{3}{4} = \frac{1}{2}$

$\frac{1}{2} \times \frac{3}{10} = \frac{3}{20}$

$\frac{3}{4} \times \frac{2}{9} = \frac{3}{18}$

Saturday With Spike

Name _____ Date _____

Read.
Solve each problem on another sheet of paper.
Write each answer in simplest form in the blank.

1. Spike spends all day Saturday working for his dog-walking service. Spike spends $\frac{2}{3}$ day walking dogs. He spends $\frac{1}{4}$ of that time walking large dogs. What part of a day does Spike spend walking large dogs?

   _____ day

2. Spike's friend Fifi spends $\frac{1}{2}$ day working for Spike. She spends $\frac{3}{4}$ of that time walking poodles. What part of a day does Fifi spend walking poodles?

   _____ day

3. Spike uses $\frac{4}{5}$ gallon of water for dogs to drink. He gives $\frac{1}{4}$ of that water to the small dogs. What part of the gallon does he give to the small dogs?

   _____ gallon

4. Of all the dogs that Spike is walking, $\frac{1}{3}$ are not first-time walkers. Of that number, $\frac{3}{4}$ of the dogs have walked with Spike two or more times. What part of the group of dogs that Spike is walking have walked with him two or more times?

   _____ group

5. Fifi is collecting information on the group of dogs that Spike walks. She recorded that $\frac{7}{10}$ of the dogs are male and $\frac{2}{3}$ of those male dogs are puppies. What part of the group of dogs that Spike walks are male puppies?

   _____ group

6. Fifi also noted that $\frac{5}{6}$ of the poodles that she walks are white. Of those white poodles, $\frac{1}{2}$ are female. What part of the group of poodles that Fifi walks are white females?

   _____ group

It's Not Easy!

Name _____ Date _____

Multiply.
Show your work.
Write each answer in simplest form.
Color the matching answer on the giraffe.
Some answers will not be colored.

$7 \times \frac{1}{5} =$

$\frac{1}{4} \times 9 =$

$\frac{2}{3} \times 4 =$

$\frac{3}{4} \times 6 =$

$\frac{1}{2} \times 4 =$

$3 \times \frac{5}{8} =$

$\frac{3}{5} \times 5 =$

$6 \times \frac{2}{7} =$

$2 \times \frac{7}{8} =$

$\frac{4}{5} \times 7 =$

$\frac{1}{3} \times 5 =$

$\frac{2}{9} \times 8 =$

$\frac{3}{10} \times 9 =$

$\frac{1}{8} \times 2 =$

$\frac{1}{6} \times 3 =$

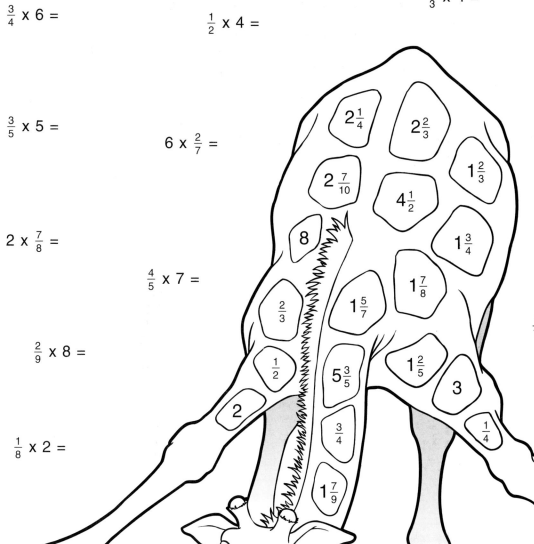

$2\frac{1}{4}$ $2\frac{2}{3}$ $1\frac{2}{3}$ $2\frac{7}{10}$ $4\frac{1}{2}$ 8 $1\frac{3}{4}$ $\frac{2}{3}$ $1\frac{7}{8}$ $1\frac{5}{7}$ $\frac{1}{2}$ $5\frac{3}{5}$ $1\frac{2}{5}$ 2 3 $\frac{3}{4}$ $\frac{1}{4}$ $1\frac{7}{9}$

Anyone have an extra **long** straw?

No More Milk

Name _____   Date _____

Multiply.
Show your work.
Write each answer in simplest form.

A $\frac{1}{3} \times 9 =$

N $10 \times \frac{1}{4} =$

S $\frac{1}{4} \times 7 =$

H $\frac{2}{5} \times 7 =$

D $5 \times \frac{3}{8} =$

E $\frac{3}{5} \times 2 =$

I $\frac{5}{6} \times 6 =$

R $3 \times \frac{1}{9} =$

U $\frac{2}{7} \times 14 =$

A $4 \times \frac{7}{8} =$

E $8 \times \frac{3}{7} =$

R $\frac{1}{5} \times 12 =$

L $\frac{4}{5} \times 6 =$

S $3 \times \frac{1}{12} =$

W $\frac{4}{9} \times 4 =$

U $5 \times \frac{1}{10} =$

D $15 \times \frac{2}{3} =$

E $\frac{3}{4} \times 8 =$

A $\frac{1}{8} \times 3 =$

F $9 \times \frac{4}{7} =$

Did you hear about the cow without any milk?
To solve the riddle, write the letters above on the matching lines below.

"__ __ __   __ __ __   __ __"
$1\frac{3}{4}$ $2\frac{4}{5}$ 6 $1\frac{7}{9}$ 3 $\frac{1}{4}$ $3\frac{1}{2}$ $2\frac{1}{2}$

__ __ __ __ __   __ __ __ __ __ __ __ __ __ __!
$\frac{1}{2}$ $1\frac{7}{8}$ 10 $3\frac{3}{7}$ $\frac{1}{3}$ $5\frac{1}{7}$ $\frac{3}{8}$ 5 $4\frac{4}{5}$ 4 $2\frac{2}{5}$ $1\frac{1}{5}$

Let's Salsa!

Multiply.
Show your work on another sheet of paper.
Write each answer in simplest form.
Color the pepper red if correct and green if incorrect.

$\frac{3}{4} \times 6 = 4\frac{1}{2}$

$9 \times \frac{1}{6} = 1\frac{1}{2}$

$\frac{1}{3} \times 12 = 4$

$\frac{2}{5} \times 15 = 6$

$7 \times \frac{4}{5} = 4\frac{3}{5}$

$\frac{3}{8} \times 9 = 3\frac{5}{8}$

$\frac{5}{8} \times 8 = \frac{5}{64}$

$\frac{1}{12} \times 4 = \frac{1}{3}$

$5 \times \frac{1}{4} = 1\frac{1}{4}$

$\frac{1}{8} \times 5 = \frac{5}{8}$

$3 \times \frac{3}{5} = 1\frac{4}{5}$

$\frac{7}{8} \times 2 = 1\frac{3}{4}$

$14 \times \frac{1}{4} = 4\frac{1}{2}$

$\frac{7}{10} \times 10 = 7$

$15 \times \frac{1}{5} = 3$

$\frac{2}{7} \times 3 = \frac{2}{21}$

$3 \times \frac{2}{3} = 2$

$\frac{1}{9} \times 3 = \frac{1}{27}$

$\frac{4}{9} \times 7 = 3\frac{2}{9}$

$\frac{9}{10} \times 3 = 2\frac{7}{10}$

©The Education Center, Inc. • *Target Math Success* • TEC60833 • Key p. 133

Lana's Library

Name _____   Date _____

Read.
Solve each problem on another
sheet of paper.
Write your answer in simplest
form in the blank.

Just Buggy!

1. Lana has collected
enough books to
create her very own
library. She has 15
books about bugs
and $\frac{2}{3}$ of those
books are about
lightning bugs. How
many of Lana's bug
books are about
lightning bugs?

_____ books

2. The top shelf of Lana's bookshelf has 8
books on it. Picture books make up $\frac{1}{4}$
of those books. How many of the books
on the top shelf are picture books?

_____ books

3. Lana's library shelves are 12 inches
long. Books cover $\frac{4}{5}$ the length of each
shelf. How many inches of each shelf
are covered with books?

_____ inches

How to Shine Brighter

4. Larry borrowed 8 books from
Lana's library. He has returned
$\frac{3}{4}$ of those books. How many
books has Larry returned?

_____ books

5. Lana read 16 books this week. Of
all the books Lana read, $\frac{1}{4}$ were
adventure books. How many of
the books that Lana read this
week were adventure books?

_____ books

6. Lana wants to add
20 new books to
her library in the
next year. She
wants $\frac{1}{5}$ of the new
books to be about
the outdoors. How
many new books
does Lana want
to be about the
outdoors?

_____ books

The Light of My Life

Leaving a Trail

Name _____ Date _____

Multiply.
Show your work.
Write each answer in simplest form.

$\frac{5}{12}$ x $1\frac{1}{2}$ = _____

$\frac{1}{2}$ x $1\frac{5}{8}$ = _____

$\frac{2}{5}$ x $4\frac{1}{6}$ = _____

$\frac{1}{4}$ x $2\frac{1}{3}$ = _____

$\frac{3}{10}$ x $5\frac{2}{3}$ = _____

$\frac{1}{7}$ x $3\frac{5}{6}$ = _____

$\frac{1}{5}$ x $6\frac{1}{8}$ = _____

$\frac{4}{5}$ x $1\frac{3}{7}$ = _____

$\frac{1}{4}$ x $3\frac{3}{5}$ = _____

$\frac{2}{9}$ x $1\frac{4}{5}$ = _____

$\frac{1}{8}$ x $2\frac{2}{5}$ = _____

$\frac{3}{8}$ x $4\frac{1}{3}$ = _____

$\frac{3}{4}$ x $2\frac{1}{6}$ = _____

$\frac{1}{9}$ x $4\frac{1}{2}$ = _____

Multiplying fractions by mixed numbers 69

Sail Away!

Name _____ Date _____

Multiply.
Show your work.
Write each answer in simplest form.
Color by the code.

$\frac{1}{2}$ x $12\frac{2}{7}$ =

$\frac{5}{6}$ x $2\frac{1}{4}$ =

$\frac{3}{4}$ x $4\frac{4}{9}$ =

$\frac{1}{5}$ x $2\frac{1}{3}$ =

$\frac{2}{3}$ x $5\frac{3}{7}$ =

$\frac{1}{8}$ x $1\frac{1}{10}$ =

$\frac{1}{4}$ x $3\frac{5}{7}$ =

$\frac{3}{8}$ x $7\frac{1}{9}$ =

$\frac{1}{3}$ x $15\frac{3}{4}$ =

$\frac{6}{7}$ x $10\frac{1}{2}$ =

$\frac{5}{12}$ x $14\frac{1}{4}$ =

$\frac{4}{9}$ x $11\frac{2}{5}$ =

$\frac{5}{8}$ x $8\frac{2}{3}$ =

$\frac{3}{10}$ x $1\frac{1}{6}$ =

Jumpin' Joeys

Name _____ Date _____

Multiply.
Show your work.
Color if correct to show the path to the trampoline.

Start

$\frac{2}{5}$ x $1\frac{5}{12}$ = $\frac{15}{30}$	$\frac{3}{8}$ x $4\frac{5}{6}$ = $1\frac{13}{16}$	$\frac{4}{7}$ x $3\frac{1}{2}$ = 2
$\frac{1}{6}$ x $6\frac{2}{9}$ = $1\frac{1}{27}$	$\frac{4}{5}$ x $2\frac{1}{10}$ = $1\frac{2}{5}$	$\frac{2}{3}$ x $9\frac{6}{7}$ = $6\frac{1}{7}$	$\frac{1}{4}$ x $7\frac{4}{9}$ = $1\frac{3}{6}$
$\frac{11}{12}$ x $3\frac{1}{3}$ = $3\frac{1}{3}$	$\frac{5}{8}$ x $8\frac{3}{10}$ = $5\frac{3}{16}$	$\frac{3}{4}$ x $1\frac{11}{12}$ = $1\frac{7}{16}$	$\frac{1}{8}$ x $9\frac{3}{5}$ = $1\frac{1}{5}$
$\frac{1}{2}$ x $12\frac{4}{9}$ = $12\frac{2}{9}$	$\frac{3}{5}$ x $5\frac{2}{3}$ = $3\frac{1}{5}$	$\frac{7}{12}$ x $6\frac{1}{4}$ = $3\frac{3}{4}$	$\frac{5}{6}$ x $4\frac{2}{7}$ = $3\frac{4}{7}$
$\frac{3}{8}$ x $11\frac{1}{5}$ = $4\frac{2}{5}$	$\frac{5}{7}$ x $13\frac{1}{2}$ = $9\frac{9}{14}$	$\frac{1}{3}$ x $8\frac{7}{10}$ = $2\frac{9}{10}$	$\frac{3}{4}$ x $7\frac{1}{6}$ = $5\frac{5}{6}$
	$\frac{9}{10}$ x $2\frac{5}{8}$ = $2\frac{29}{80}$	$\frac{2}{5}$ x $11\frac{3}{7}$ = $14\frac{3}{7}$	$\frac{5}{8}$ x $9\frac{3}{4}$ = $6\frac{3}{16}$

Multiplying fractions by mixed numbers 71

Too Many T-Shirts!

Name _____ Date _____

Read.
Solve each problem on another sheet of paper.
Write each answer in simplest form in the blank provided.

1.
Zoe has been collecting T-shirts for almost ten years. She has $6\frac{3}{4}$ dozens of T-shirts. Zoe has outgrown $\frac{1}{3}$ of her T-shirts. How many dozens of T-shirts has Zoe outgrown?

_____ dozens

2.
Zoe's T-shirts fill $3\frac{1}{4}$ boxes. If she empties $\frac{2}{5}$ of those boxes, how many boxes will Zoe empty?

_____ boxes

3.
Zoe has gotten $1\frac{5}{6}$ dozens of T-shirts from sports camps. Of her camp T-shirts, $\frac{3}{8}$ are from soccer camps. How many dozens of T-shirts did Zoe get from soccer camps?

_____ dozens

4.
Zoe's oldest T-shirt is $9\frac{1}{6}$ years old. Her favorite T-shirt is $\frac{1}{2}$ as old as her oldest. How old is Zoe's favorite T-shirt?

_____ years old

5.
Zoe has decided to give away $3\frac{1}{8}$ dozens of T-shirts. She wants to give $\frac{3}{5}$ of the shirts to her cousins. How many dozens of T-shirts will Zoe give to her cousins?

_____ dozens

6.
Zoe will have $3\frac{5}{8}$ dozens of T-shirts left. She is hoping to keep $\frac{2}{3}$ of those T-shirts for ten more years. How many dozens of T-shirts does Zoe hope to keep for ten more years?

_____ dozens

A Meal Made for a Musician

Name _____   Date _____

Multiply.
Show your work on another sheet
  of paper.
Write each answer in simplest form.

P: $6\frac{1}{4} \times 3\frac{1}{5} =$

S: $1\frac{1}{7} \times 2\frac{1}{3} =$

L: $1\frac{1}{5} \times 2\frac{1}{2} =$

H: $3\frac{1}{9} \times 1\frac{1}{4} =$

E: $3\frac{1}{2} \times 2\frac{1}{7} =$

T: $2\frac{1}{6} \times 1\frac{1}{2} =$

E: $2\frac{1}{8} \times 1\frac{1}{3} =$

L: $1\frac{2}{9} \times 1\frac{7}{11} =$

A: $3\frac{3}{4} \times 2\frac{2}{5} =$

O: $5\frac{1}{6} \times 1\frac{1}{3} =$

O: $5\frac{1}{2} \times 1\frac{1}{3} =$

F: $8\frac{1}{8} \times 3\frac{1}{5} =$

T: $2\frac{6}{7} \times 2\frac{1}{10} =$

U: $2\frac{1}{7} \times 2\frac{1}{10} =$

E: $7\frac{1}{3} \times 1\frac{1}{8} =$

I need a spoon!

What did the musician eat for breakfast?
To solve the riddle, match the letters above to the numbered lines below.

____ ____ ____ ____ ____
$3\frac{8}{9}$ $7\frac{1}{2}$ 9   6 $2\frac{5}{6}$

"____ ____ ____ ____ ____ ____ ____ ____ ____ ____"
26 2 $4\frac{1}{2}$ $3\frac{1}{4}$ $8\frac{1}{4}$ 3 $7\frac{1}{3}$ $6\frac{8}{9}$ 20 $2\frac{2}{3}$.

Multiplying mixed numbers

Cheer Gear

Name _____ Date _____

Multiply.
Show your work.
Write each answer in simplest form.

$2\frac{1}{7} \times 1\frac{1}{3} =$

$1\frac{1}{10} \times 3\frac{1}{3} =$

$2\frac{1}{4} \times 3\frac{1}{3} =$

$2\frac{6}{7} \times 2\frac{1}{5} =$

$3\frac{1}{2} \times 3\frac{1}{7} =$

$4\frac{1}{5} \times 4\frac{1}{6} =$

$6\frac{3}{4} \times 1\frac{1}{9} =$

$1\frac{1}{2} \times 1\frac{2}{3} =$

$5\frac{2}{5} \times 2\frac{1}{3} =$

$2\frac{2}{3} \times 3\frac{1}{8} =$

$6\frac{1}{2} \times 1\frac{1}{2} =$

$1\frac{1}{8} \times 5\frac{1}{9} =$

$4\frac{2}{5} \times 2\frac{3}{11} =$

$1\frac{1}{9} \times 1\frac{1}{5} =$

$1\frac{1}{5} \times 3\frac{1}{2} =$

$1\frac{1}{11} \times 1\frac{1}{6} =$

Multiplying mixed numbers

All You Can Eat

Name _____ Date _____

Multiply.
Show your work.
Write each answer in simplest form.
Color the boxes with answers less than 20 to show the path to the buffet.

3-6-09

Start

$3\frac{1}{5} \times 2\frac{1}{8} =$

$2\frac{7}{12} \times 4\frac{4}{5} =$

$9\frac{1}{6} \times 2\frac{1}{15} =$

$9\frac{5}{8} \times 4\frac{2}{7} =$

$11\frac{1}{6} \times 2\frac{1}{3} =$

$6\frac{1}{9} \times 3\frac{9}{10} =$

$4\frac{2}{7} \times 4\frac{1}{12} =$

$17\frac{1}{2} \times 3\frac{3}{5} =$

$21\frac{1}{2} \times 1\frac{7}{12} =$

$1\frac{1}{2} \times 11\frac{9}{10} =$

$3\frac{1}{16} \times 2\frac{2}{5} =$

$8\frac{4}{7} \times 3\frac{1}{3} =$

$8\frac{1}{4} \times 6\frac{2}{3} =$

$5\frac{1}{11} \times 3\frac{1}{7} =$

BAMBOO BUFFET

Multiplying mixed numbers

Track and Field Feats

Name _____   Date _____

Read.
Show your work on another sheet of paper.
Write each answer in simplest form in the blank.

1. At the Gazelles On-the-Go track meet, Gage ran $1\frac{1}{2}$ kilometers. Gail ran $3\frac{1}{3}$ times as far as Gage. How far did Gail run?

   _____ kilometers

2. In the long jump, Gary jumped $2\frac{1}{4}$ meters. Gina jumped $1\frac{5}{6}$ times that distance. How far did Gina jump?

   _____ meters

3. Ginger jumped a height of $5\frac{1}{5}$ meters in the pole vault event. George jumped $2\frac{1}{4}$ times higher than Ginger. How high did George jump?

   _____ meters

4. During the next event, Gail threw the javelin $6\frac{1}{8}$ meters. Gage threw it $3\frac{3}{5}$ times farther than Gail. How far did Gage throw the javelin?

   _____ meters

5. Gary threw the discus $8\frac{3}{4}$ meters. Gina threw $4\frac{1}{10}$ times as far as Gary. How far did Gina throw the discus?

   _____ meters

6. The last event was the triple jump. George jumped $3\frac{1}{10}$ meters. Ginger jumped $2\frac{6}{7}$ times farther than George. How far did Ginger jump?

   _____ meters

©The Education Center, Inc. • *Target Math Success* • TEC60833 • Key p. 134

Story problems: multiplying mixed numbers

Dividing Fractions

Dividing Fractions

Table of Contents

Parent Communication and Student Checkups

See pages 116–123 for corresponding parent communications and student checkups (mini tests) for the skills listed above.

Team Spirit

Divide.
Show your work.
Write each answer in simplest form.

Give me a D!

$5 \div \frac{3}{5} =$

$3 \div \frac{1}{3} =$

$4 \div \frac{3}{8} =$

$6 \div \frac{1}{4} =$

$2 \div \frac{3}{4} =$

$9 \div \frac{1}{6} =$

$8 \div \frac{2}{3} =$

$7 \div \frac{1}{2} =$

$1 \div \frac{6}{7} =$

$12 \div \frac{5}{6} =$

It's All Downhill From Here!

Name _____ Date _____

Divide.
Show your work.
Write each answer in simplest form.
Cross off the matching answer in the answer bank.
Some answers will not be crossed off.

$1 \div \frac{5}{7} =$

$7 \div \frac{1}{5} =$

$12 \div \frac{1}{2} =$

$10 \div \frac{2}{5} =$

$4 \div \frac{2}{3} =$

$5 \div \frac{3}{8} =$

$2 \div \frac{3}{4} =$

$26 \div \frac{1}{3} =$

$8 \div \frac{5}{6} =$

$15 \div \frac{3}{10} =$

$20 \div \frac{1}{4} =$

$9 \div \frac{1}{6} =$

$3 \div \frac{2}{9} =$

$13 \div \frac{5}{8} =$

$14 \div \frac{1}{8} =$

$12 \div \frac{4}{5} =$

$11 \div \frac{3}{5} =$

$16 \div \frac{1}{10} =$

Answer Bank

4	$13\frac{1}{2}$
15	6
$1\frac{2}{5}$	$18\frac{1}{3}$
54	$9\frac{3}{5}$
6	35
$1\frac{3}{4}$	160
78	$13\frac{1}{3}$
25	80
112	$2\frac{2}{3}$
50	24
	$20\frac{4}{5}$

Dividing a whole number by a fraction

Where's My Bone?

Name _____ Date _____

Divide.
Show your work on another sheet of paper.
Color if correct.
Connect the colored boxes to show the path to the bone.

I know I buried it here somewhere!

Start

$\frac{1}{2} \div 9 = \frac{1}{18}$

$\frac{1}{4} \div 3 = 12$

$\frac{2}{5} \div 8 = 3\frac{1}{5}$

$\frac{1}{8} \div 4 = 2$

$\frac{3}{7} \div 11 = \frac{3}{77}$

$\frac{5}{8} \div 12 = \frac{5}{96}$

$\frac{2}{3} \div 12 = \frac{1}{18}$

$\frac{1}{12} \div 5 = \frac{5}{12}$

$\frac{3}{4} \div 5 = \frac{3}{20}$

$\frac{1}{3} \div 10 = 3\frac{1}{3}$

$\frac{9}{10} \div 7 = \frac{9}{70}$

$\frac{1}{6} \div 9 = 1\frac{1}{2}$

$\frac{4}{5} \div 10 = 8$

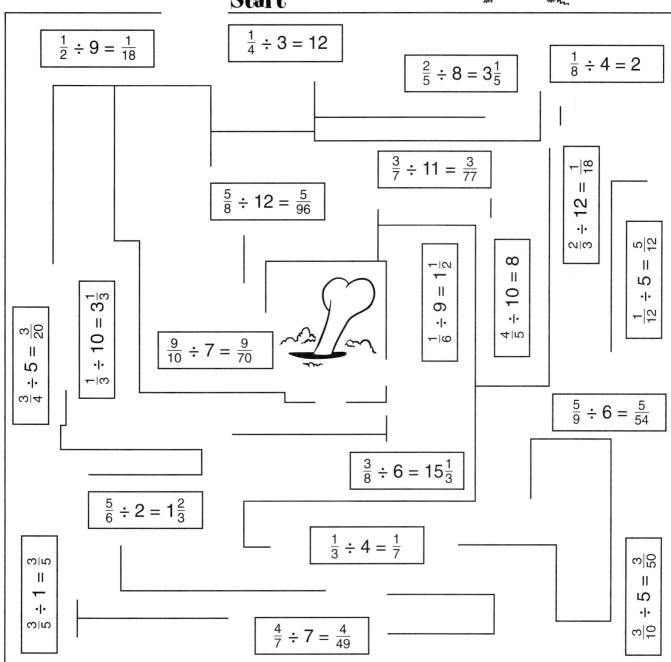

$\frac{5}{9} \div 6 = \frac{5}{54}$

$\frac{3}{8} \div 6 = 15\frac{1}{3}$

$\frac{5}{6} \div 2 = 1\frac{2}{3}$

$\frac{1}{3} \div 4 = \frac{1}{7}$

$\frac{3}{5} \div 1 = 3\frac{1}{5}$

$\frac{3}{10} \div 5 = \frac{3}{50}$

$\frac{4}{7} \div 7 = \frac{4}{49}$

Dividing a fraction by a whole number **81**

Bumper Boat Blunder

Name _____ Date _____

Divide.
Show your work on another sheet of paper.
Write each answer in simplest form.

(D) $\frac{1}{3} \div 3 =$ (P) $\frac{3}{8} \div 5 =$

(I) $\frac{11}{12} \div 2 =$ (O) $\frac{1}{6} \div 7 =$ (T) $\frac{4}{9} \div 4 =$

What did the dolphin say when she bumped into the pelican?

(D) $\frac{3}{5} \div 10 =$ (I) $\frac{9}{10} \div 3 =$ (T) $\frac{5}{8} \div 6 =$

(I) $\frac{2}{3} \div 8 =$ (I) $\frac{7}{12} \div 1 =$ (N) $\frac{1}{2} \div 13 =$ (E) $\frac{3}{4} \div 12 =$

(O) $\frac{1}{4} \div 9 =$ (D) $\frac{5}{6} \div 5 =$ (R) $\frac{1}{8} \div 7 =$ (O) $\frac{7}{10} \div 4 =$

(S) $\frac{6}{7} \div 6 =$ (N) $\frac{2}{5} \div 10 =$ (O) $\frac{1}{12} \div 8 =$ (P) $\frac{3}{8} \div 9 =$

To answer the riddle, match the letters above to the answers below.

$$\overline{\frac{11}{24}} \quad \overline{\frac{3}{50}} \quad \overline{\frac{7}{12}} \quad \overline{\frac{1}{9}} \quad \overline{\frac{1}{25}} \quad \overline{\frac{5}{48}} \quad {}^{,} \quad \overline{\frac{1}{6}} \quad \overline{\frac{1}{42}} \quad \overline{\frac{3}{10}} \quad \overline{\frac{1}{9}}$$

$$\overline{\frac{7}{40}} \quad \overline{\frac{1}{26}} \quad {}^{\text{“}} \quad \overline{\frac{3}{40}} \quad \overline{\frac{1}{96}} \quad \overline{\frac{1}{56}} \quad \overline{\frac{1}{24}} \quad \overline{\frac{1}{36}} \quad \overline{\frac{1}{12}} \quad \overline{\frac{1}{7}} \quad \overline{\frac{1}{16}} \quad {}^{\text{”}} .$$

Dividing a fraction by a whole number

"A-moose-ment" Park Fun

Name _____ Date _____

Read.
Show your work on another sheet of paper.
Write each answer in simplest form in the blank provided.

1. Matt earned 5 free tickets to Moose Mountain by selling candy bars. If he earned $\frac{1}{3}$ of a ticket for every candy bar he sold, how many candy bars did Matt sell?

   _____ candy bars

2. Matt and his family plan to spend 6 hours at the park. They decide to meet at the Ice Creamery every $\frac{2}{3}$ of an hour to check in. How many times do Matt and his family plan to meet?

   _____ times

3. Matt and Maria stood in line for 18 minutes before they got to ride the Cliffs roller coaster. The ride lasted $\frac{3}{4}$ of a minute. How many times could Matt and Maria have ridden the Cliffs during the time they were standing in line?

   _____ times

4. The Cliffs roller coaster has 2 miles of track. There is either a steep climb, a fast drop, or a sharp turn every $\frac{1}{8}$ of a mile. How many times does the track climb, drop, or turn?

   _____ times

5. Matt bought 3 pounds of peanuts to share with his family. If they ate $\frac{4}{5}$ of a pound every hour, how long would the peanuts last?

   _____ hours

6. There are 8 miles of paths at Moose Mountain. Drink stands are stationed every $\frac{2}{5}$ of a mile. How many drink stands are there in Moose Mountain?

   _____ drink stands

Birthday Bash Crash

Name _____   Date _____

Read.
Show your work on another sheet of paper.
Write each answer in simplest form in the blank provided.

1.
Cindy had $\frac{1}{2}$ of a pizza left after her birthday party. She gave the pizza to 5 friends.
How much pizza did each friend get?

_____ of the pizza

2.
There was $\frac{5}{6}$ of a gallon of punch left after the party. If Cindy's 3 brothers each drink an equal amount, how much punch will each one of them drink?

_____ of a gallon

3.
After the party, $\frac{1}{3}$ of the cake was left. Cindy gave it to her 3 brothers. How much cake did each brother get?

_____ of the cake

4.
Cindy found that $\frac{3}{5}$ of the balloons had not popped. She handed out the balloons to 6 of her neighbors. What part of the balloons did each neighbor get?

_____ of the balloons

5.
It took Cindy $\frac{3}{4}$ of an hour to clean up the 2 rooms used for the party. How long did it take to clean each room?

_____ of an hour

6.
Cindy spent $\frac{1}{4}$ of the next day writing thank-you notes. She wrote 6 notes. How long did it take Cindy to write each note?

_____ of the day

Story problems: dividing a fraction by a whole number

Bird's-Eye View

Name _____ Date _____

Divide.
Show your work.
Write each answer in simplest form.

What a great shot!

$\frac{1}{4} \div \frac{1}{8} =$

$\frac{3}{7} \div \frac{1}{5} =$

$\frac{2}{3} \div \frac{1}{6} =$

$\frac{3}{8} \div \frac{1}{12} =$

$\frac{3}{10} \div \frac{1}{9} =$

$\frac{1}{2} \div \frac{7}{8} =$

$\frac{4}{5} \div \frac{3}{4} =$

$\frac{7}{12} \div \frac{1}{3} =$

$\frac{8}{15} \div \frac{2}{9} =$

$\frac{4}{11} \div \frac{2}{7} =$

$\frac{5}{6} \div \frac{1}{16} =$

$\frac{5}{6} \div \frac{2}{3} =$

$\frac{2}{3} \div \frac{4}{15} =$

$\frac{7}{8} \div \frac{3}{4} =$

Desert Oasis

Name _____ Date _____

Divide.
Show your work.
Write each answer in simplest form.
Color the boxes with answers greater than 5 to show the path to the drink stand's entrance.

$\frac{7}{8} \div \frac{1}{12} =$ Start	$\frac{1}{2} \div \frac{1}{16} =$	$\frac{9}{10} \div \frac{1}{6} =$
$\frac{9}{10} \div \frac{3}{5} =$	$\frac{1}{6} \div \frac{1}{3} =$	$\frac{3}{4} \div \frac{3}{8} =$	$\frac{7}{9} \div \frac{1}{15} =$
$\frac{10}{21} \div \frac{1}{6} =$	$\frac{5}{6} \div \frac{3}{8} =$	$\frac{13}{14} \div \frac{2}{21} =$	$\frac{11}{12} \div \frac{1}{8} =$
$\frac{5}{6} \div \frac{1}{4} =$	$\frac{14}{15} \div \frac{2}{3} =$	$\frac{11}{16} \div \frac{1}{8} =$	

OASIS

Water......................5¢
Lemonade...............10¢

Dividing a fraction by a fraction

Polar Pops

Name _____ Date _____

Divide.
Show your work.
Write each answer in simplest form.
Cross off the answer on the polar bear.
Some numbers will not be crossed off.

$\dfrac{3}{4} \div \dfrac{1}{2} =$ $\dfrac{5}{6} \div \dfrac{1}{3} =$

$\dfrac{1}{8} \div \dfrac{3}{4} =$ $\dfrac{4}{5} \div \dfrac{1}{10} =$

$\dfrac{5}{8} \div \dfrac{10}{17} =$ $\dfrac{3}{5} \div \dfrac{9}{14} =$

$\dfrac{6}{7} \div \dfrac{1}{14} =$ $\dfrac{7}{9} \div \dfrac{1}{6} =$

$\dfrac{7}{8} \div \dfrac{1}{2} =$ $\dfrac{4}{5} \div \dfrac{1}{4} =$

$\dfrac{3}{8} \div \dfrac{9}{10} =$ $\dfrac{2}{3} \div \dfrac{7}{15} =$

$\dfrac{19}{20} \div \dfrac{3}{10} =$ $\dfrac{7}{10} \div \dfrac{1}{5} =$

$\dfrac{2}{3} \div \dfrac{2}{15} =$ $\dfrac{9}{14} \div \dfrac{1}{7} =$

$\dfrac{8}{9} \div \dfrac{1}{6} =$

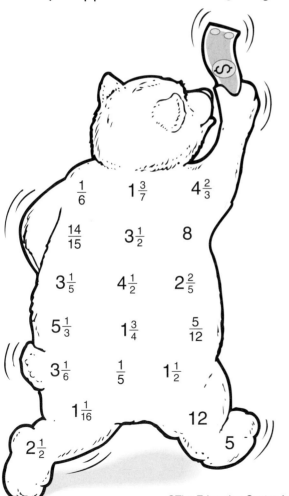

$\dfrac{1}{6}$ $1\dfrac{3}{7}$ $4\dfrac{2}{3}$

$\dfrac{14}{15}$ $3\dfrac{1}{2}$ 8

$3\dfrac{1}{5}$ $4\dfrac{1}{2}$ $2\dfrac{2}{5}$

$5\dfrac{1}{3}$ $1\dfrac{3}{4}$ $\dfrac{5}{12}$

$3\dfrac{1}{6}$ $\dfrac{1}{5}$ $1\dfrac{1}{2}$

$1\dfrac{1}{16}$ 12

$2\dfrac{1}{2}$ 5

Cool Cat Costumes

Name _____ Date _____

Read.
Show your work on another sheet of paper.
Write each answer in simplest form in the blank.

COOL CAT COSTUME SHOP

1. At the Cool Cat Costume Shop, Chris is making lion costumes. He has $\frac{1}{2}$ of a yard of felt. If he needs $\frac{1}{4}$ of a yard of felt for each costume, how many costumes can he make?

   _____ costumes

2. Carol is cutting material for milkman costumes. She has $\frac{1}{5}$ of a yard of cotton. If she needs $\frac{1}{15}$ of a yard of cotton for each shirt, how many shirts can she make?

   _____ shirts

3. Carl is gluing together orange foam for cheese costumes. He has $\frac{7}{8}$ of a yard of foam and needs $\frac{1}{8}$ of a yard for each costume. How many costumes can he make?

   _____ costumes

4. Callie is working on special dogcatcher costumes for some of her friends. She has $\frac{1}{3}$ of a yard of brown material. If she needs $\frac{1}{9}$ of a yard of material for each pair of pants, how many pairs of pants can she make?

   _____ pairs

5. Clay is making nets for fisherman costumes. He has $\frac{2}{3}$ of a yard of netting. If he needs $\frac{1}{12}$ of a yard of netting for each net, how many nets can he make?

   _____ nets

6. Caroline is measuring material for the fisherman costumes. She has $\frac{5}{6}$ of a yard of fabric for the shirts. If she needs $\frac{1}{12}$ of a yard of fabric for each shirt, how many shirts can she make?

   _____ shirts

Story problems: dividing a fraction by a fraction

Don't "Bee" Late!

Name _____ Date _____

3-6-09

Divide.
Show your work.
Write each answer in simplest form.

 T $4\frac{1}{2} \div 1\frac{1}{2} =$

 H $3\frac{1}{3} \div 2\frac{2}{3} =$

 **Z** $3\frac{1}{7} \div 1\frac{4}{7} =$

 H $3\frac{1}{4} \div 1\frac{1}{8} =$

 A $5\frac{1}{2} \div 1\frac{1}{6} =$

 E $2\frac{1}{2} \div 2\frac{1}{4} =$

 E $4\frac{1}{8} \div 3\frac{2}{3} =$

 K $3\frac{2}{5} \div 1\frac{1}{5} =$

 B $4\frac{1}{2} \div 1\frac{7}{8} =$

 T $2\frac{1}{10} \div 1\frac{2}{5} =$

 E $2\frac{2}{3} \div 1\frac{1}{6} =$

 S $2\frac{2}{5} \div 1\frac{1}{3} =$

BUSY BEE SCHOOL

Z $3\frac{3}{4} \div 1\frac{1}{8} =$

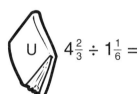 **U** $4\frac{2}{3} \div 1\frac{1}{6} =$

How does the bee get to school each day?

To solve the riddle, match the letters above to the numbered lines below.

$$\underline{\quad}\;\underline{\quad}\qquad \underline{\quad}\;\underline{\quad}\;\underline{\quad}\;\underline{\quad}\;\underline{\quad}\qquad \underline{\quad}\;\underline{\quad}\;\underline{\quad}\qquad ``\underline{\quad}\;\underline{\quad}\;\underline{\quad}\;\underline{\quad}"\,!$$

$2\frac{8}{9}\quad 2\frac{2}{7}\qquad 3\quad 4\frac{5}{7}\quad 2\frac{5}{6}\quad 1\frac{1}{8}\quad 1\frac{4}{5}\qquad 1\frac{1}{2}\quad 1\frac{1}{4}\quad 1\frac{1}{9}\qquad 2\frac{2}{5}\quad 4\quad 3\frac{1}{3}\quad 2$

Dividing mixed numbers

Surf's Up!

Name _____ Date _____

Divide.
Show your work.
Write each answer in simplest form.

Kowabunga!

Color Code
greater than 4 = blue
between 2 and 4 = yellow
less than 2 = green

$4\frac{1}{2} \div 1\frac{1}{5} =$

$2\frac{3}{5} \div 2\frac{1}{6} =$

$6\frac{2}{5} \div 1\frac{1}{3} =$

$8\frac{1}{3} \div 1\frac{7}{8} =$

$11\frac{2}{3} \div 2\frac{1}{2} =$

$3\frac{1}{3} \div 1\frac{1}{6} =$

$7\frac{1}{2} \div 1\frac{1}{4} =$

$5\frac{1}{4} \div 1\frac{3}{8} =$

$4\frac{2}{3} \div 1\frac{3}{4} =$

$6\frac{1}{4} \div 1\frac{2}{3} =$

$3\frac{1}{3} \div 2\frac{6}{7} =$

$4\frac{2}{3} \div 1\frac{2}{5} =$

$5\frac{1}{5} \div 3\frac{1}{4} =$

$5\frac{1}{4} \div 1\frac{3}{4} =$

$10\frac{2}{3} \div 1\frac{5}{6} =$

$13\frac{1}{2} \div 2\frac{1}{4} =$

A "Reel-y" Good Movie

Name _____ Date _____

Divide.
Show your work.
Write each answer in simplest form.
Color the popcorn piece with the matching
   answer.
Some popcorn pieces will not be colored.

$3\frac{2}{5} \div 1\frac{1}{10} =$

$10\frac{1}{2} \div 2\frac{1}{3} =$

$6\frac{1}{2} \div 3\frac{1}{2} =$

$4\frac{1}{2} \div 2\frac{2}{5} =$

$7\frac{1}{7} \div 3\frac{1}{3} =$

$3\frac{1}{2} \div 1\frac{3}{11} =$

$11\frac{2}{3} \div 1\frac{2}{3} =$

$5\frac{3}{5} \div 4\frac{2}{3} =$

$8\frac{4}{5} \div 2\frac{4}{9} =$

$8\frac{4}{7} \div 6\frac{2}{3} =$

$6\frac{4}{5} \div 4\frac{1}{4} =$

$7\frac{1}{5} \div 2\frac{4}{7} =$

$6\frac{3}{7} \div 4\frac{1}{2} =$

$9\frac{1}{3} \div 5\frac{3}{5} =$

$6\frac{3}{4} \div 1\frac{1}{8} =$

$10\frac{1}{2} \div 4\frac{2}{3} =$

$6\frac{3}{4} \div 4\frac{1}{2} =$

$7\frac{1}{3} \div 2\frac{3}{4} =$

POPCORN

7    $2\frac{2}{3}$ $1\frac{2}{7}$

$2\frac{1}{7}$ $4\frac{1}{2}$

$1\frac{3}{7}$

$2\frac{1}{4}$ $2\frac{4}{5}$

$6\frac{1}{2}$

$1\frac{5}{9}$

$2\frac{3}{4}$ $1\frac{3}{5}$

$1\frac{7}{8}$

$3\frac{3}{5}$

$1\frac{1}{2}$

$3\frac{1}{11}$

6    $1\frac{2}{3}$

5

$1\frac{6}{7}$ $1\frac{1}{5}$

POPCORN

Digging the Vacation

Name _____ Date _____

Read.
Show your work on another sheet of paper.
Write each answer in simplest form in the blank.

1. The Dalmatian family drove to the beach for a vacation. The family drove $10\frac{1}{2}$ hours to get there. If the family took a break every $3\frac{1}{2}$ hours, how many times did they stop? _____ times

2. On the first day, Dexter and his sister Dolly were on the beach for $5\frac{1}{4}$ hours. They jumped in the water every $1\frac{3}{4}$ hours. How many times did they jump in the water? _____ times

3. On the same day, Dexter's dad fished for $5\frac{1}{2}$ hours. If he caught a fish every $2\frac{3}{4}$ hours, how many fish did he catch? _____ fish

4. On the second day, Dexter and Dolly were on the beach for $5\frac{3}{5}$ hours. If they dug a hole every $1\frac{2}{5}$ hours, how many holes did they dig? _____ holes

5. While Dexter and Dolly were on the beach for $5\frac{3}{5}$ hours, their mom took them a snack every $2\frac{4}{5}$ hours. How many times did she give them a snack? _____ times

6. On the third day, the family was on the beach for $7\frac{1}{2}$ hours. If they put sunscreen on their noses every $2\frac{1}{2}$ hours, how many times did they use sunscreen? _____ times

©The Education Center, Inc. • *Target Math Success* • TEC60833 • Key p. 135

Story problems: dividing mixed numbers

Parent Communication and Student Checkups

Parent Communication and Student Checkups

Table of Contents

How to Administer the Checkups

The checkups will help you determine which students have mastered a skill and which students may need more practice.

You Hit the Bull's-Eye!

_____

has mastered **multiplying and dividing fractions.**

_____
Teacher

_____
Date

You Hit the Mark!

_____

has mastered **adding and subtracting fractions.**

_____
Teacher

_____
Date

It's Time to Take Aim!

On _____ our class will be having a checkup on fractions. To help your child prepare, please spend about 20 minutes reviewing math problems that involve **finding equivalent fractions and simplest form.** Thanks for your help!

Fractions Refresher

Need help explaining equivalent fractions and simplest form to your child? Try using the method below. Walk your child through the first problem in each section at the right using this method. Next, have him complete the second problem on his own, verbalizing each step as he solves the problem. Then have him complete the remaining problems independently.

Finding Equivalent Fractions

Multiply the numerator and the denominator by the same number.

$$\frac{1}{4} = \frac{1 \times 3}{4 \times 3} = \frac{3}{12}$$

$\frac{1}{4}$ and $\frac{3}{12}$ are equivalent fractions.

Finding Simplest Form
Step 1
Do: List all of the factors of both the numerator and the denominator.
Ask: Are there any common factors besides 1? *(Yes)*

$\frac{8}{12}$ (factors: 1, **2, 4,** 8)
      (factors: 1, **2,** 3, **4,** 6, 12)

Step 2
Do: Divide the numerator and the denominator by a common factor until the fraction is in its simplest form.
Ask: Are there any common factors besides 1? *(No)*

$$\frac{8}{12} = \frac{8 \div 2}{12 \div 2} = \frac{4}{6} = \frac{4 \div 2}{6 \div 2} = \frac{2}{3}$$

The simplest form of $\frac{8}{12}$ is $\frac{2}{3}$.

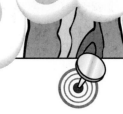

Try this method!

Target These!

Write an equivalent fraction.

1. $\frac{1}{4} =$ 2. $\frac{1}{2} =$

3. $\frac{3}{4} =$ 4. $\frac{2}{5} =$

5. $\frac{3}{7} =$ 6. $\frac{5}{6} =$

Write each fraction in simplest form.

1. $\frac{8}{12} =$ 2. $\frac{9}{27} =$

3. $\frac{30}{42} =$ 4. $\frac{18}{30} =$

5. $\frac{8}{32} =$ 6. $\frac{15}{24} =$

Simplest form:
$\frac{2}{3}, \frac{1}{3}, \frac{5}{7}, \frac{3}{5}, \frac{1}{4}, \frac{5}{8}$

for equivalent forms:
$\frac{1}{4} = \frac{2}{12}, \frac{1}{2} = \frac{2}{4}, \frac{3}{4} = \frac{8}{8},$
$\frac{2}{5} = \frac{6}{15}, \frac{3}{7} = \frac{6}{14}, \frac{5}{6} = \frac{15}{18}$

Answers: Possible answers

If your child is quick to solve the remaining math problems correctly, an occasional review may be all he or she needs. But if several of the answers are incorrect, it's a good idea to spend some time each day having your child work through a problem or two at home until he or she has mastered this skill.

Checkup 1

Name _____ Date _____

Write an equivalent fraction.

A. $\frac{1}{2} =$ $\frac{3}{8} =$ $\frac{4}{5} =$ $\frac{2}{3} =$

B. $\frac{3}{4} =$ $\frac{1}{6} =$ $\frac{5}{7} =$ $\frac{4}{9} =$

C. $\frac{7}{10} =$ $\frac{5}{6} =$

Test A: Equivalent fractions

©The Education Center, Inc. • *Target Math Success* • TEC60833 • Key p. 135

97

Checkup 1

Name _____ Date _____

Write the fraction in simplest form.

A. $\frac{25}{30} =$ $\frac{8}{32} =$ $\frac{20}{32} =$ $\frac{6}{18} =$

B. $\frac{35}{40} =$ $\frac{14}{28} =$ $\frac{12}{27} =$ $\frac{10}{15} =$

C. $\frac{24}{40} =$ $\frac{54}{63} =$

Test B: Simplest form

©The Education Center, Inc. • *Target Math Success* • TEC60833 • Key p. 135

It's Time to Take Aim!

On _____ our class will be having a checkup on fractions. To help your child prepare, please spend about 20 minutes reviewing math problems that involve **adding or subtracting fractions with like denominators.** Thanks for your help!

Fractions Refresher

Need help explaining to your child how to add or subtract fractions with like denominators? Try using the two-step method below. Walk your child through the first problem at the right using this method. Next, have her complete the second problem on her own, verbalizing each step as she solves the problem. Then have her complete the remaining problems independently.

Adding or Subtracting Fractions With Like Denominators

Step 1
Add or subtract the numerators. Write the sum or difference over the common denominator.

$$+ \frac{\frac{3}{8}}{\frac{1}{8}} = \frac{4}{8}$$

Step 2
Write the answer in simplest form.

$$\frac{4}{8} = \frac{1}{2}$$

Try these two steps!

Target These!

1. $\frac{3}{8}$ 2. $\frac{2}{5}$
   $+ \frac{1}{8}$ $+ \frac{1}{5}$

3. $\frac{1}{6} + \frac{1}{6} =$

4. $\frac{1}{3} + \frac{1}{3} =$

5. $\frac{4}{7} + \frac{2}{7} =$

6. $\frac{9}{10}$ 7. $\frac{5}{8}$
   $- \frac{3}{10}$ $- \frac{1}{8}$

8. $\frac{5}{6} - \frac{1}{6} =$

9. $\frac{4}{5} - \frac{1}{5} =$

10. $\frac{2}{3} - \frac{1}{3} =$

Answers: 1. $\frac{1}{2}$, 2. $\frac{3}{5}$, 3. $\frac{1}{3}$, 4. $\frac{2}{3}$, 5. $\frac{6}{7}$, 6. $\frac{3}{5}$, 7. $\frac{1}{2}$, 8. $\frac{2}{3}$, 9. $\frac{3}{5}$, 10. $\frac{1}{3}$

If your child is quick to solve the remaining math problems correctly, an occasional review may be all he or she needs. But if several of the answers are incorrect, it's a good idea to spend some time each day having your child work through a problem or two at home until he or she has mastered this skill.

Checkup 2

Name _____   Date _____

A.
$$\frac{2}{7}$$
$$+\frac{3}{7}$$

B.
$$\frac{3}{10}$$
$$+\frac{1}{10}$$

C. $\frac{3}{8} + \frac{3}{8} =$

D. $\frac{5}{7} + \frac{1}{7} =$

Test A: Adding fractions with like denominators

Checkup 2

Name _____   Date _____

A.
$$\frac{5}{8}$$
$$-\frac{3}{8}$$

B.
$$\frac{4}{5}$$
$$-\frac{1}{5}$$

C. $\frac{8}{9} - \frac{1}{9} =$

D. $\frac{11}{12} - \frac{5}{12} =$

A.
$$\frac{6}{7}$$
$$-\frac{2}{7}$$

B.
$$\frac{5}{6}$$
$$-\frac{1}{6}$$

A.
$$\frac{7}{10}$$
$$-\frac{3}{10}$$

C. $\frac{5}{8} - \frac{1}{8} =$

D. $\frac{3}{5} - \frac{2}{5} =$

Test B: Subtracting fractions with like denominators

It's Time to Take Aim!

On _____ our class will be having a checkup on fractions. To help your child prepare, please spend about 20 minutes reviewing math problems that involve **adding or subtracting fractions with unlike denominators.** Thanks for your help!

Fractions Refresher

Need help explaining to your child how to add or subtract fractions with unlike denominators? Try using the three-step method below. Walk your child through the first problem at the right using this method. Next, have him complete the second problem on his own, verbalizing each step as he solves the problem. Then have him complete the remaining problems independently.

Step 1
Rewrite the fractions with a common denominator.

$$\frac{1}{2} \quad \frac{1 \times 3}{2 \times 3} = \frac{3}{6}$$
$$+\frac{1}{6} \quad \frac{1 \times 1}{6 \times 1} = \frac{1}{6}$$

Step 2
Add or subtract the numerators. Write the sum or difference over the common denominator.

$$\frac{3}{6}$$
$$+\frac{1}{6}$$
$$\frac{4}{6}$$

Step 3
Write the answer in simplest form.

$$\frac{4}{6} = \frac{2}{3}$$

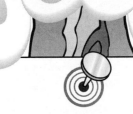

Target These!

1. $\frac{1}{2}$
   $+ \frac{1}{6}$

2. $\frac{2}{5}$
   $+ \frac{1}{3}$

3. $\frac{2}{7}$
   $+ \frac{1}{2}$

4. $\frac{2}{9}$
   $+ \frac{2}{3}$

5. $\frac{3}{8}$
   $+ \frac{1}{2}$

6. $\frac{7}{9}$
   $- \frac{1}{6}$

7. $\frac{2}{3}$
   $- \frac{1}{8}$

8. $\frac{4}{7}$
   $- \frac{3}{14}$

9. $\frac{4}{5}$
   $- \frac{1}{3}$

10. $\frac{6}{7}$
    $- \frac{3}{14}$

Try these three steps!

If your child is quick to solve the remaining math problems correctly, an occasional review may be all he or she needs. But if several of the answers are incorrect, it's a good idea to spend some time each day having your child work through a problem or two at home until he or she has mastered this skill.

Checkup 3

Checkup 3

Name _____ Date _____

Name _____ Date _____

(Right worksheet)

A. $\frac{5}{8}$ $-\frac{1}{4}$

$\frac{6}{7}$ $-\frac{1}{2}$

$\frac{8}{9}$ $-\frac{2}{3}$

B. $\frac{4}{5}$ $-\frac{1}{2}$

$\frac{11}{12}$ $-\frac{3}{4}$

$\frac{5}{7}$ $-\frac{1}{6}$

C. $\frac{1}{2} - \frac{1}{3} =$

$\frac{7}{10} - \frac{1}{4} =$

D. $\frac{7}{8} - \frac{2}{3} =$

$\frac{9}{11} - \frac{1}{2} =$

Test B: Subtracting fractions with unlike denominators

(Left worksheet)

A. $\frac{1}{3}$ $+\frac{3}{8}$

$\frac{1}{2}$ $+\frac{1}{9}$

$\frac{2}{5}$ $+\frac{1}{4}$

B. $\frac{1}{2}$ $+\frac{1}{4}$

$\frac{3}{7}$ $+\frac{1}{3}$

$\frac{1}{6}$ $+\frac{3}{10}$

C. $\frac{7}{10} + \frac{1}{8} =$

$\frac{1}{4} + \frac{4}{7} =$

D. $\frac{1}{12} + \frac{3}{8} =$

$\frac{1}{15} + \frac{2}{3} =$

Test A: Adding fractions with unlike denominators

It's Time to Take Aim!

On _____ our class will be having a checkup on fractions. To help your child prepare, please spend about 20 minutes reviewing math problems that involve **adding and subtracting mixed numbers with like and unlike denominators.** Thanks for your help!

Fractions Refresher

Need help explaining to your child how to add or subtract mixed numbers with like and unlike denominators? Try using the three-step method below. Walk your child through the first problem at the right using this method. Next, have her complete the second problem on her own, verbalizing each step as she solves the problem. Then have her complete the remaining problems independently.

Step 1

Rewrite the fractions with common denominators.

$$3\frac{1}{5} \qquad \frac{1}{5} = \frac{2}{10}$$
$$+ 2\frac{3}{10} \qquad \frac{3}{10} = \frac{3}{10}$$

Step 2

Add or subtract the numerators. Write the sum or difference over the common denominator. Add or subtract the whole numbers.

$$3\frac{2}{10}$$
$$+ 2\frac{3}{10}$$
$$\overline{5\frac{5}{10}}$$

Step 3

Write the answer in simplest form.

$$5\frac{5}{10} = 5\frac{1}{2}$$

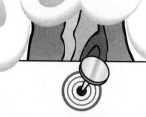

Try using these three steps!

Target These!

1. $3\frac{1}{5}$
    $+ 2\frac{3}{10}$

2. $1\frac{1}{6}$
    $+ 5\frac{1}{6}$

3. $4\frac{1}{8}$
    $+ 2\frac{3}{4}$

4. $6\frac{1}{9}$
    $+ 7\frac{2}{9}$

5. $2\frac{1}{3}$
    $+ 4\frac{1}{5}$

6. $3\frac{7}{8}$
    $- 2\frac{1}{8}$

7. $7\frac{4}{9}$
    $- 1\frac{1}{3}$

8. $11\frac{5}{12}$
    $- 3\frac{1}{12}$

9. $8\frac{6}{7}$
    $- 6\frac{2}{3}$

10. $8\frac{4}{5}$
    $- 2\frac{1}{5}$

Answers: $5\frac{1}{2}$, $6\frac{1}{3}$, $6\frac{7}{8}$, $13\frac{1}{3}$, $6\frac{8}{15}$, $1\frac{3}{4}$, $6\frac{1}{9}$, $8\frac{1}{3}$, $2\frac{4}{21}$, $6\frac{3}{5}$

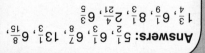

If your child is quick to solve the remaining math problems correctly, an occasional review may be all he or she needs. But if several of the answers are incorrect, it's a good idea to spend some time each day having your child work through a problem or two at home until he or she has mastered this skill.

Checkup 4

A.
$$2\tfrac{1}{4} + 3\tfrac{5}{8} \qquad 5\tfrac{4}{7} + 2\tfrac{1}{7} \qquad 6\tfrac{3}{8} + 5\tfrac{1}{6}$$

B.
$$3\tfrac{4}{9} + 7\tfrac{1}{9} \qquad 2\tfrac{1}{5} + 4\tfrac{2}{7} \qquad 8\tfrac{1}{3} + 9\tfrac{1}{3}$$

C. $6\tfrac{2}{9} + 3\tfrac{1}{4} =$ $\qquad$ $7\tfrac{1}{10} + 8\tfrac{1}{10} =$

D. $4\tfrac{3}{4} + 5\tfrac{1}{6} =$ $\qquad$ $2\tfrac{1}{12} + 9\tfrac{1}{12} =$

Test A: Adding mixed numbers with like and unlike denominators

---

Checkup 4

A.
$$10\tfrac{1}{2} - 5\tfrac{1}{4} \qquad 7\tfrac{7}{8} - 3\tfrac{1}{8} \qquad 4\tfrac{5}{9} - 2\tfrac{1}{3}$$

B.
$$13\tfrac{4}{5} - 7\tfrac{1}{5} \qquad 9\tfrac{11}{12} - 8\tfrac{3}{4} \qquad 11\tfrac{7}{10} - 3\tfrac{1}{10}$$

C. $14\tfrac{3}{4} - 12\tfrac{1}{6} =$ $\qquad$ $5\tfrac{1}{3} - 4\tfrac{1}{3} =$

D. $9\tfrac{7}{8} - 6\tfrac{2}{3} =$ $\qquad$ $11\tfrac{8}{15} - 4\tfrac{2}{15} =$

Test B: Subtracting mixed numbers with like and unlike denominators

It's Time to Take Aim!

On _____ our class will be having a checkup on fractions. To help your child prepare, please spend about 20 minutes reviewing math problems that involve **subtracting mixed numbers with like and unlike denominators with regrouping.** Thanks for your help!

Fractions Refresher

Need help explaining to your child how to subtract mixed numbers with like and unlike denominators with regrouping? Try using the four-step method below. Walk your child through the first problem at the right using this method. Next, have him complete the second problem on his own, verbalizing each step as he solves the problem. Then have him complete the remaining problems independently.

Step 1
Ask: Are the denominators the same? *(No)*
Do: Rewrite the fractions with a common denominator.

$$3\frac{1}{6} = 3\frac{1}{6}$$
$$-2\frac{2}{3} = -2\frac{4}{6}$$

Step 2
Ask: Do I need to regroup? *(Yes)*
Do: Borrow one whole fraction and rewrite the mixed number.

$$3\frac{1}{6} = 2\frac{7}{6} \leftarrow \frac{1}{6} + \frac{6}{6} = \frac{7}{6}$$
$$-2\frac{4}{6} = -2\frac{4}{6}$$

Step 3
Subtract the fractions. Subtract the whole numbers.

$$2\frac{7}{6}$$
$$-2\frac{4}{6}$$
$$\overline{0\frac{3}{6}}$$

Step 4
Write the answer in simplest form.

$$\frac{3}{6} = \frac{1}{2}$$

1. $3\frac{1}{6}$
   $-2\frac{2}{3}$

2. $4\frac{2}{5}$
   $-1\frac{3}{5}$

3. $3\frac{1}{6}$
   $-2\frac{1}{4}$

4. $6\frac{3}{7}$
   $-4\frac{4}{5}$

5. $7\frac{2}{3}$
   $-3\frac{9}{10}$

6. $12\frac{1}{8}$
   $-3\frac{3}{8}$

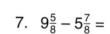

7. $9\frac{5}{8} - 5\frac{7}{8} =$

8. $20\frac{5}{6} - 8\frac{9}{10} =$

9. $11\frac{1}{3} - 10\frac{2}{3} =$

10. $6\frac{2}{7} - 1\frac{1}{2} =$

Answers: $\frac{1}{2}$; $2\frac{4}{5}$; $\frac{11}{12}$; $1\frac{22}{35}$; $3\frac{23}{30}$; $8\frac{3}{4}$; $3\frac{3}{4}$; $11\frac{14}{15}$; $\frac{2}{3}$; $4\frac{11}{14}$

If your child is quick to solve the remaining math problems correctly, an occasional review may be all he or she needs. But if several of the answers are incorrect, it's a good idea to spend some time each day having your child work through a problem or two at home until he or she has mastered this skill.

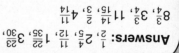

Checkup 5

Name _____ Date _____

A.
$$5\tfrac{1}{4} - 3\tfrac{1}{3}$$
$$2\tfrac{5}{6} - 1\tfrac{9}{10}$$

B.
$$7\tfrac{1}{5} - 4\tfrac{4}{5}$$
$$10\tfrac{2}{3} - 3\tfrac{6}{7}$$

C.
$$9\tfrac{1}{8} - 1\tfrac{1}{2} =$$
$$7\tfrac{2}{5} - 5\tfrac{2}{3} =$$

D.
$$10\tfrac{1}{6} - 8\tfrac{3}{8} =$$
$$3\tfrac{1}{9} - 2\tfrac{1}{8} =$$

Test A: Subtracting mixed numbers with like and unlike denominators with regrouping

---

Checkup 5

Name _____ Date _____

A.
$$6\tfrac{1}{2} - 4\tfrac{5}{8}$$
$$3\tfrac{1}{3} - 1\tfrac{6}{7}$$
$$9\tfrac{2}{5} - 5\tfrac{7}{10}$$

B.
$$7\tfrac{3}{4} - 2\tfrac{5}{6}$$
$$11\tfrac{1}{4} - 3\tfrac{2}{3}$$
$$8\tfrac{1}{5} - 4\tfrac{3}{8}$$

C.
$$10\tfrac{4}{7} - 1\tfrac{2}{3} =$$
$$8\tfrac{2}{9} - 5\tfrac{1}{2} =$$

D.
$$6\tfrac{3}{5} - 1\tfrac{4}{5} =$$
$$15\tfrac{1}{10} - 5\tfrac{3}{5} =$$

Test B: Subtracting mixed numbers with like and unlike denominators with regrouping

It's Time to Take Aim!

On _____ our class will be having a checkup on fractions. To help your child prepare, please spend about 20 minutes reviewing math problems that involve **subtracting fractions from whole numbers or mixed numbers.** Thanks for your help!

Fractions Refresher

Need help explaining to your child how to subtract fractions from whole numbers or mixed numbers? Try using the methods below. Walk your child through the first problem at the right using the first method. Next, have her complete the second problem on her own, verbalizing each step as she solves the problem. Then have her complete the third, fourth, and fifth problems independently. Repeat the process with problems 6–10 using the second method.

Subtracting a fraction from a whole number:

Step 1
Rename the whole number.

$$3 = 2\frac{2}{2}$$
$$-\frac{1}{2} = -\frac{1}{2}$$

Step 2
Subtract the fractions. Then subtract the whole numbers.

$$2\frac{2}{2}$$
$$-\frac{1}{2}$$
$$2\frac{1}{2}$$

Step 3
Write the answer in simplest form.
$$2\frac{1}{2}$$

Subtracting a fraction from a mixed number:

Step 1
Rewrite the fraction using a common denominator.

$$3\frac{1}{6} = 3\frac{1}{6}$$
$$-\frac{1}{2} = -\frac{3}{6}$$

Step 2
Rename the mixed number if needed.

$$3\frac{1}{6} = 2\frac{6}{6} + \frac{1}{6} = 2\frac{7}{6}$$
$$-\frac{3}{6} = -\frac{3}{6} = -\frac{3}{6}$$

Step 3
Subtract the fractions.

$$2\frac{7}{6}$$
$$-\frac{3}{6}$$
$$2\frac{4}{6}$$

Step 4
Write the answer in simplest form.
$$2\frac{4}{6} = 2\frac{2}{3}$$

Try using these steps!

Target These!

1. 3
$-\frac{1}{2}$

2. 6
$-\frac{7}{9}$

3. 1
$-\frac{2}{5}$

4. 5
$-\frac{1}{10}$

5. 3
$-\frac{1}{6}$

6. $3\frac{1}{6}$
$-\frac{1}{2}$

7. $7\frac{1}{3}$
$-\frac{5}{9}$

8. $4\frac{1}{3}$
$-\frac{7}{8}$

9. $7\frac{1}{10}$
$-\frac{5}{6}$

10. $8\frac{1}{8}$
$-\frac{3}{4}$

Answers: $2\frac{1}{2}$; $5\frac{2}{9}$; $\frac{3}{5}$; $4\frac{9}{10}$; $2\frac{5}{6}$; $2\frac{2}{3}$; $6\frac{7}{9}$; $3\frac{11}{24}$; $6\frac{4}{15}$; $7\frac{3}{8}$

If your child is quick to solve the remaining math problems correctly, an occasional review may be all he or she needs. But if several of the answers are incorrect, it's a good idea to spend some time each day having your child work through a problem or two at home until he or she has mastered this skill.

Checkup 6

Name _____ Date _____

A. $7 - \frac{4}{5}$ $5 - \frac{1}{8}$

B. $10 - \frac{1}{5}$ $11 - \frac{7}{10}$

C. $8 - \frac{1}{3} =$

D. $12 - \frac{3}{4} =$

Test A: Subtracting fractions from whole numbers

©The Education Center, Inc. • *Target Math Success* • TEC60833 • Key p. 136

Checkup 6

Name _____ Date _____

A. $3\frac{5}{7} - \frac{2}{7}$ $6\frac{1}{4} - \frac{3}{8}$ $5\frac{1}{8} - \frac{7}{8}$

B. $2\frac{1}{3} - \frac{5}{6}$ $11\frac{3}{5} - \frac{4}{5}$ $9\frac{7}{9} - \frac{1}{9}$

C. $4\frac{5}{7} - \frac{1}{2} =$ $10\frac{3}{10} - \frac{4}{5} =$

D. $2\frac{1}{8} - \frac{3}{8} =$ $7\frac{2}{3} - \frac{2}{5} =$

Test B: Subtracting fractions from mixed numbers

©The Education Center, Inc. • *Target Math Success* • TEC60833 • Key p. 136

It's Time to Take Aim!

On _____ our class will be having a checkup on fractions. To help your child prepare, please spend about 20 minutes reviewing math problems that involve **multiplying fractions by fractions.** Thanks for your help!

Fractions Refresher

Need help explaining to your child how to multiply fractions by fractions? Try using the two-step method below. Walk your child through the first problem at the right using this method. Next, have him complete the second problem on his own, verbalizing each step as he solves the problem. Then have him complete the remaining problems independently.

Step 1
Multiply the numerators. Multiply the denominators.

$$\frac{1}{3} \times \frac{3}{4} = \frac{3}{12}$$

Step 2
Write the answer in simplest form.

$$\frac{3}{12} = \frac{1}{4}$$

Try using these two steps!

Target These!

1. $\frac{1}{3} \times \frac{3}{4} =$ 2. $\frac{1}{5} \times \frac{1}{2} =$

3. $\frac{2}{5} \times \frac{1}{4} =$ 4. $\frac{1}{3} \times \frac{2}{3} =$

5. $\frac{5}{6} \times \frac{3}{4} =$ 6. $\frac{2}{9} \times \frac{2}{3} =$

7. $\frac{7}{8} \times \frac{1}{2} =$ 8. $\frac{2}{7} \times \frac{1}{8} =$

9. $\frac{1}{6} \times \frac{2}{3} =$

10. $\frac{3}{8} \times \frac{4}{5} =$

Answers: $\frac{1}{4}$, $\frac{1}{10}$, $\frac{1}{10}$, $\frac{2}{9}$, $\frac{5}{8}$, $\frac{4}{27}$, $\frac{7}{16}$, $\frac{1}{28}$, $\frac{1}{9}$, $\frac{3}{10}$

If your child is quick to solve the remaining math problems correctly, an occasional review may be all he or she needs. But if several of the answers are incorrect, it's a good idea to spend some time each day having your child work through a problem or two at home until he or she has mastered this skill.

Checkup 7

Name _____ Date _____

A. $\dfrac{1}{8} \times \dfrac{2}{3} =$ $\dfrac{3}{5} \times \dfrac{1}{2} =$ $\dfrac{1}{4} \times \dfrac{4}{5} =$

B. $\dfrac{1}{5} \times \dfrac{5}{8} =$ $\dfrac{2}{5} \times \dfrac{1}{10} =$ $\dfrac{1}{3} \times \dfrac{3}{7} =$

C. $\dfrac{4}{7} \times \dfrac{3}{8} =$ $\dfrac{1}{6} \times \dfrac{4}{9} =$

D. $\dfrac{7}{8} \times \dfrac{2}{9} =$ $\dfrac{3}{10} \times \dfrac{1}{2} =$

Test A: Multiplying fractions by fractions

Checkup 7

Name _____ Date _____

A. $\dfrac{5}{9} \times \dfrac{3}{5} =$ $\dfrac{1}{7} \times \dfrac{7}{9} =$ $\dfrac{1}{4} \times \dfrac{3}{4} =$

B. $\dfrac{5}{6} \times \dfrac{3}{10} =$ $\dfrac{2}{7} \times \dfrac{3}{8} =$ $\dfrac{2}{5} \times \dfrac{1}{6} =$

C. $\dfrac{2}{3} \times \dfrac{7}{10} =$ $\dfrac{9}{10} \times \dfrac{1}{3} =$

D. $\dfrac{2}{5} \times \dfrac{5}{8} =$ $\dfrac{1}{9} \times \dfrac{4}{7} =$

Test B: Multiplying fractions by fractions

It's Time to Take Aim!

On _____ our class will be having a checkup on fractions. To help your child prepare, please spend about 20 minutes reviewing math problems that involve **multiplying fractions by whole numbers.** Thanks for your help!

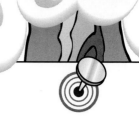

Target These!

1. $4 \times \frac{5}{6} =$ 2. $3 \times \frac{2}{3} =$

3. $\frac{7}{8} \times 6 =$ 4. $5 \times \frac{1}{10} =$

5. $8 \times \frac{5}{6} =$ 6. $\frac{5}{7} \times 7 =$

7. $\frac{4}{5} \times 2 =$ 8. $9 \times \frac{3}{7} =$

9. $\frac{1}{7} \times 5 =$

10. $6 \times \frac{3}{4} =$

Fractions Refresher

Need help explaining to your child how to multiply fractions and whole numbers? Try using the three-step method below. Walk your child through the first problem at the right using this method. Next, have her complete the second problem on her own, verbalizing each step as she solves the problem. Then have her complete the remaining problems independently.

Try these three steps!

Step 1
Rewrite the whole number as a fraction with 1 as the denominator.

$$4 \times \frac{5}{6} =$$

$$\frac{4}{1} \times \frac{5}{6} =$$

Step 2
Multiply the numerators. Multiply the denominators.

$$\frac{4}{1} \times \frac{5}{6} = \frac{20}{6}$$

Step 3
Write the answer in simplest form.

$$\frac{20}{6} = 3\frac{2}{6} = 3\frac{1}{3}$$

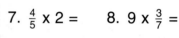

Answers: $3\frac{1}{3}$, 2, $5\frac{1}{4}$, $6\frac{2}{3}$, 5, $1\frac{3}{5}$, $3\frac{6}{7}$, 4$\frac{1}{2}$

If your child is quick to solve the remaining math problems correctly, an occasional review may be all he or she needs. But if several of the answers are incorrect, it's a good idea to spend some time each day having your child work through a problem or two at home until he or she has mastered this skill.

Checkup 8

Name _____

Date _____

A. $\dfrac{1}{3} \times 5 =$ $6 \times \dfrac{1}{8} =$

B. $3 \times \dfrac{4}{9} =$ $\dfrac{5}{6} \times 8 =$

C. $\dfrac{3}{4} \times 2 =$ $3 \times \dfrac{3}{10} =$

D. $\dfrac{2}{9} \times 5 =$ $4 \times \dfrac{3}{4} =$

Test A: Multiplying fractions by whole numbers

Checkup 8

Name _____

Date _____

A. $4 \times \dfrac{1}{8} =$ $\dfrac{3}{5} \times 5 =$

B. $\dfrac{5}{7} \times 7 =$ $3 \times \dfrac{4}{5} =$

C. $\dfrac{5}{8} \times 4 =$ $9 \times \dfrac{2}{5} =$

D. $6 \times \dfrac{1}{2} =$ $\dfrac{1}{4} \times 10 =$

Test B: Multiplying fractions by whole numbers

It's Time to Take Aim!

On _____ our class will be having a checkup on multiplication of fractions. To help your child prepare, please spend about 20 minutes reviewing math problems that involve **multiplying fractions by mixed numbers.** Thanks for your help!

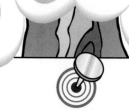

Target These!

1. $\frac{2}{3} \times 1\frac{1}{4} =$

2. $\frac{3}{10} \times 2\frac{2}{5} =$

3. $\frac{5}{12} \times 3\frac{1}{2} =$

4. $\frac{4}{7} \times 8\frac{2}{3} =$

5. $\frac{3}{8} \times 4\frac{1}{6} =$

6. $\frac{7}{9} \times 1\frac{4}{5} =$

7. $\frac{3}{4} \times 7\frac{1}{8} =$

8. $\frac{1}{5} \times 6\frac{7}{10} =$

9. $\frac{5}{6} \times 9\frac{1}{9} =$

10. $\frac{1}{4} \times 3\frac{11}{12} =$

Fractions Refresher

Need help explaining to your child how to multiply fractions by mixed numbers? Try using the three-step method below. Walk your child through the first problem at the right using this method. Next, have him complete the second problem on his own, verbalizing each step as he solves the problem. Then have him complete the remaining problems independently.

Step 1
Change the mixed number into an improper fraction.

$$\frac{2}{3} \times 1\frac{1}{4} =$$

$$\frac{2}{3} \times \frac{5}{4} =$$

Step 2
Multiply the numerators. Multiply the denominators.

$$\frac{2}{3} \times \frac{5}{4} = \frac{10}{12}$$

Step 3
Write the answer in simplest form.

$$\frac{10}{12} = \frac{5}{6}$$

Try using these three steps!

Answers: $\frac{5}{6}$; $\frac{18}{25}$; $1\frac{11}{24}$; $4\frac{20}{21}$; $1\frac{9}{16}$; $1\frac{2}{5}$; $5\frac{11}{32}$; $1\frac{17}{50}$; $7\frac{27}{48}$; $\frac{47}{48}$

If your child is quick to solve the remaining math problems correctly, an occasional review may be all he or she needs. But if several of the answers are incorrect, it's a good idea to spend some time each day having your child work through a problem or two at home until he or she has mastered this skill.

Checkup 9

Name _____ Date _____

A. $\frac{1}{5} \times 6\frac{1}{3} =$

B. $\frac{1}{2} \times 9\frac{1}{6} =$

C. $\frac{3}{4} \times 8\frac{3}{7} =$

D. $\frac{5}{8} \times 4\frac{1}{9} =$

E. $\frac{5}{12} \times 1\frac{1}{8} =$

Checkup 9

Name _____ Date _____

A. $\frac{4}{9} \times 5\frac{3}{10} =$

B. $\frac{5}{7} \times 1\frac{4}{15} =$

C. $\frac{4}{5} \times 7\frac{1}{8} =$

D. $\frac{1}{6} \times 8\frac{9}{10} =$

E. $\frac{3}{4} \times 9\frac{1}{3} =$

It's Time to Take Aim!

On _____ our class will be having a checkup on fractions. To help your child prepare, please spend about 20 minutes reviewing math problems that involve **multiplying a mixed number by a mixed number.** Thanks for your help!

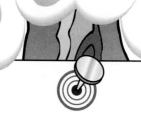

Target These!

1. $2\frac{1}{5} \times 1\frac{1}{4} =$

2. $1\frac{1}{5} \times 2\frac{1}{2} =$

3. $3\frac{1}{7} \times 1\frac{1}{4} =$

4. $5\frac{1}{4} \times 1\frac{1}{7} =$

5. $2\frac{1}{6} \times 1\frac{2}{3} =$

6. $6\frac{1}{2} \times 1\frac{1}{7} =$

7. $2\frac{4}{5} \times 2\frac{1}{7} =$

8. $1\frac{2}{3} \times 2\frac{1}{8} =$

9. $2\frac{3}{4} \times 1\frac{1}{2} =$

10. $1\frac{2}{5} \times 2\frac{1}{6} =$

Fractions Refresher

Need help explaining to your child how to multiply mixed numbers? Try using the four-step method below. Walk your child through the first problem at the right using this method. Next, have her complete the second problem on her own, verbalizing each step as she solves the problem. Then have her complete the remaining problems independently.

Try using these four steps!

Step 1
Write each mixed number as an improper fraction.

$$2\frac{1}{5} \times 1\frac{1}{4} = \frac{11}{5} \times \frac{5}{4}$$

Step 2
Simplify using the greatest common factor (GCF) if possible.

$$\frac{11}{\underset{1}{5}} \times \frac{\overset{1}{5}}{4}$$

Step 3
Multiply.

$$\frac{11}{1} \times \frac{1}{4} = \frac{11}{4}$$

Step 4
Rewrite the improper fraction as a mixed number in simplest form.

$$\frac{11}{4} = 2\frac{3}{4}$$

Answers: $2\frac{3}{4}$, 3, $3\frac{13}{14}$, 6, $3\frac{11}{18}$, $7\frac{3}{7}$, 6, $3\frac{13}{24}$, $4\frac{1}{8}$, $3\frac{1}{30}$

If your child is quick to solve the remaining math problems correctly, an occasional review may be all he or she needs. But if several of the answers are incorrect, it's a good idea to spend some time each day having your child work through a problem or two at home until he or she has mastered this skill.

Checkup 10

Name _____

Date _____

A. $3\frac{1}{2} \times 1\frac{1}{7} =$ $1\frac{1}{5} \times 3\frac{1}{3} =$ $2\frac{1}{5} \times 1\frac{4}{11} =$

B. $2\frac{1}{4} \times 1\frac{1}{9} =$ $2\frac{3}{4} \times 1\frac{3}{5} =$ $1\frac{1}{6} \times 3\frac{1}{7} =$

C. $2\frac{1}{4} \times 3\frac{1}{5} =$ $2\frac{1}{10} \times 2\frac{3}{7} =$

D. $5\frac{3}{5} \times 1\frac{3}{7} =$ $1\frac{1}{8} \times 1\frac{1}{3} =$

Checkup 10

Name _____

Date _____

A. $2\frac{3}{5} \times 1\frac{2}{3} =$ $5\frac{1}{3} \times 1\frac{1}{4} =$ $3\frac{3}{5} \times 1\frac{1}{6} =$

B. $6\frac{1}{4} \times 3\frac{1}{5} =$ $2\frac{1}{2} \times 1\frac{3}{10} =$ $4\frac{1}{2} \times 1\frac{1}{9} =$

C. $2\frac{2}{5} \times 1\frac{5}{8} =$ $2\frac{4}{9} \times 1\frac{1}{2} =$

D. $9\frac{1}{3} \times 2\frac{1}{7} =$ $2\frac{1}{3} \times 1\frac{5}{17} =$

It's Time to Take Aim!

On _____ our class will be having a checkup on fractions. To help your child prepare, please spend about 20 minutes reviewing math problems that involve **dividing a whole number by a fraction.** Thanks for your help!

Fractions Refresher

Need help explaining to your child how to divide a whole number by a fraction? Try using the four-step method below. Walk your child through the first problem at the right using this method. Next, have him complete the second problem on his own, verbalizing each step as he solves the problem. Then have him complete the remaining problems independently.

Step 1
Write the whole number as a fraction with 1 as the denominator.

$$3 \div \frac{3}{5} = \frac{3}{1} \div \frac{3}{5}$$

Step 2
Write a multiplication problem by inverting the second fraction.

$$\frac{3}{1} \times \frac{5}{3}$$

Step 3
Simplify using the greatest common factor (GCF).

$$\frac{\overset{1}{\cancel{3}}}{1} \times \frac{5}{\underset{1}{\cancel{3}}}$$

Step 4
Multiply. Write the answer in simplest form.

$$\frac{1}{1} \times \frac{5}{1} = 5$$

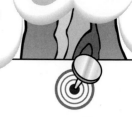

Try using these four steps!

Target These!

1. $3 \div \frac{3}{5} =$

2. $5 \div \frac{1}{10} =$

3. $2 \div \frac{3}{4} =$

4. $8 \div \frac{4}{9} =$

5. $9 \div \frac{6}{7} =$

6. $4 \div \frac{2}{3} =$

7. $6 \div \frac{3}{4} =$

8. $7 \div \frac{1}{2} =$

9. $3 \div \frac{5}{6} =$

10. $4 \div \frac{7}{8} =$

Answers: 5, 50, $2\frac{2}{3}$, 18, $10\frac{1}{2}$, 6, 8, 14, $3\frac{3}{5}$, $4\frac{4}{7}$

If your child is quick to solve the remaining math problems correctly, an occasional review may be all he or she needs. But if several of the answers are incorrect, it's a good idea to spend some time each day having your child work through a problem or two at home until he or she has mastered this skill.

Checkup 11

Name _____

Date _____

A. $2 \div \frac{3}{8} =$ $5 \div \frac{5}{7} =$ $4 \div \frac{5}{6} =$

B. $8 \div \frac{2}{3} =$ $10 \div \frac{5}{6} =$ $3 \div \frac{9}{10} =$

C. $6 \div \frac{2}{3} =$ $12 \div \frac{3}{4} =$

D. $7 \div \frac{7}{8} =$ $9 \div \frac{3}{5} =$

Test A: Dividing a whole number by a fraction

Checkup 11

Name _____

Date _____

A. $3 \div \frac{6}{7} =$ $11 \div \frac{1}{2} =$ $7 \div \frac{7}{8} =$

B. $5 \div \frac{9}{10} =$ $9 \div \frac{3}{8} =$ $10 \div \frac{2}{3} =$

C. $2 \div \frac{7}{8} =$ $4 \div \frac{2}{9} =$

D. $6 \div \frac{9}{10} =$ $8 \div \frac{5}{6} =$

Test B: Dividing a whole number by a fraction

It's Time to Take Aim!

On _____ our class will be having a checkup on fractions. To help your child prepare, please spend about 20 minutes reviewing math problems that involve **dividing a fraction by a whole number.** Thanks for your help!

Fractions Refresher

Need help explaining to your child how to divide a fraction by a whole number? Try using the four-step method below. Walk your child through the first problem at the right using this method. Next, have her complete the second problem on her own, verbalizing each step as she solves the problem. Then have her complete the remaining problems independently.

Step 1
Write the whole number as a fraction with 1 as the denominator.

$$\frac{2}{5} \div 4 = \frac{2}{5} \div \frac{4}{1}$$

Step 2
Write a multiplication problem by inverting the second fraction.

$$\frac{2}{5} \times \frac{1}{4}$$

Step 3
Simplify using the greatest common factor (GCF).

$$\frac{\overset{1}{2}}{5} \times \frac{1}{\underset{2}{4}} =$$

Step 4
Multiply. Write the answer in simplest form.

$$\frac{1}{5} \times \frac{1}{2} = \frac{1}{10}$$

Target These!

1. $\frac{2}{5} \div 4 =$

2. $\frac{3}{8} \div 6 =$

3. $\frac{1}{4} \div 8 =$

4. $\frac{2}{5} \div 3 =$

5. $\frac{5}{6} \div 10 =$

6. $\frac{1}{9} \div 2 =$

7. $\frac{5}{7} \div 4 =$

8. $\frac{1}{2} \div 7 =$

9. $\frac{2}{3} \div 6 =$

10. $\frac{5}{9} \div 5 =$

Try using these four steps!

Answers: $\frac{1}{10}, \frac{1}{16}, \frac{1}{32}, \frac{2}{15}, \frac{1}{12}, \frac{1}{18}, \frac{5}{28}, \frac{1}{14}, \frac{1}{9}, \frac{1}{9}$

If your child is quick to solve the remaining math problems correctly, an occasional review may be all he or she needs. But if several of the answers are incorrect, it's a good idea to spend some time each day having your child work through a problem or two at home until he or she has mastered this skill.

Checkup 12

Name _____

Date _____

A. $\dfrac{1}{3} \div 9 =$ $\dfrac{3}{4} \div 6 =$

B. $\dfrac{2}{5} \div 8 =$ $\dfrac{7}{8} \div 3 =$

C. $\dfrac{5}{6} \div 7 =$ $\dfrac{3}{10} \div 5 =$

D. $\dfrac{2}{3} \div 10 =$ $\dfrac{1}{4} \div 6 =$

Test A: Dividing a fraction by a whole number

Checkup 12

Name _____

Date _____

A. $\dfrac{2}{7} \div 5 =$ $\dfrac{3}{8} \div 2 =$ $\dfrac{1}{7} \div 4 =$

B. $\dfrac{1}{6} \div 3 =$ $\dfrac{4}{5} \div 12 =$ $\dfrac{7}{12} \div 2 =$

C. $\dfrac{2}{9} \div 8 =$ $\dfrac{2}{3} \div 6 =$

D. $\dfrac{1}{5} \div 11 =$ $\dfrac{1}{4} \div 9 =$

Test B: Dividing a fraction by a whole number

It's Time to Take Aim!

On _____ our class will be having a checkup on fractions. To help your child prepare, please spend about 20 minutes reviewing math problems that involve **dividing a fraction by a fraction.** Thanks for your help!

Fractions Refresher

Need help explaining to your child how to divide a fraction by a fraction? Try using the four-step method below. Walk your child through the first problem at the right using this method. Next, have him complete the second problem on his own, verbalizing each step as he solves the problem. Then have him complete the remaining problems independently.

Step 1
Invert the divisor.

$$\frac{1}{2} \div \frac{5}{8} \qquad \frac{5}{8} \longrightarrow \frac{8}{5}$$

Step 2
Rewrite the problem as a multiplication problem using the inverted fraction.

$$\frac{1}{2} \div \frac{5}{8}$$

$$\frac{1}{2} \times \frac{8}{5}$$

Step 3
Multiply.

$$\frac{1}{2} \times \frac{8}{5} = \frac{8}{10}$$

Step 4
Write the answer in simplest form.

$$\frac{8}{10} = \frac{4}{5}$$

Try using these four steps!

Target These!

1. $\frac{1}{2} \div \frac{5}{8} =$

2. $\frac{1}{5} \div \frac{1}{2} =$

3. $\frac{3}{8} \div \frac{1}{3} =$

4. $\frac{4}{5} \div \frac{1}{4} =$

5. $\frac{2}{7} \div \frac{1}{3} =$

6. $\frac{5}{8} \div \frac{3}{4} =$

7. $\frac{1}{2} \div \frac{3}{5} =$

8. $\frac{9}{10} \div \frac{1}{5} =$

9. $\frac{1}{8} \div \frac{1}{2} =$

10. $\frac{7}{12} \div \frac{2}{3} =$

Answers: $\frac{4}{5}, \frac{2}{5}, 1\frac{1}{8}, 3\frac{1}{5}, \frac{6}{7}, \frac{5}{6}, \frac{5}{6}, 4\frac{1}{2}, \frac{1}{4}, \frac{7}{8}$

If your child is quick to solve the remaining math problems correctly, an occasional review may be all he or she needs. But if several of the answers are incorrect, it's a good idea to spend some time each day having your child work through a problem or two at home until he or she has mastered this skill.

Checkup 13

Name _____ Date _____

A. $\dfrac{3}{4} \div \dfrac{1}{6} =$ $\dfrac{4}{7} \div \dfrac{1}{2} =$

B. $\dfrac{2}{3} \div \dfrac{5}{6} =$ $\dfrac{1}{4} \div \dfrac{3}{8} =$

C. $\dfrac{5}{12} \div \dfrac{1}{2} =$ $\dfrac{3}{5} \div \dfrac{5}{8} =$

D. $\dfrac{4}{5} \div \dfrac{1}{7} =$ $\dfrac{7}{12} \div \dfrac{5}{7} =$

Test A: Dividing a fraction by a fraction

Checkup 13

Name _____ Date _____

A. $\dfrac{7}{12} \div \dfrac{3}{5} =$ $\dfrac{5}{6} \div \dfrac{2}{3} =$ $\dfrac{3}{8} \div \dfrac{7}{10} =$

B. $\dfrac{5}{9} \div \dfrac{4}{5} =$ $\dfrac{1}{2} \div \dfrac{1}{12} =$ $\dfrac{6}{7} \div \dfrac{1}{4} =$

C. $\dfrac{11}{12} \div \dfrac{1}{6} =$ $\dfrac{2}{5} \div \dfrac{5}{8} =$

D. $\dfrac{3}{7} \div \dfrac{1}{8} =$ $\dfrac{5}{12} \div \dfrac{1}{5} =$

Test B: Dividing a fraction by a fraction

It's Time to Take Aim!

On _____ our class will be having a checkup on fractions. To help your child prepare, please spend about 20 minutes reviewing math problems that involve **dividing mixed numbers.** Thanks for your help!

Fractions Refresher

Need help explaining to your child how to divide mixed numbers? Try using the four-step method below. Walk your child through the first problem at the right using this method. Next, have her complete the second problem on her own, verbalizing each step as she solves the problem. Then have her complete the remaining problems independently.

Step 1
Write each mixed number as an improper fraction.

$$6\frac{2}{3} \div 2\frac{1}{2} =$$

$$\frac{20}{3} \qquad \frac{5}{2}$$

Step 2
Write a multiplication problem by inverting the second fraction.

$$\frac{20}{3} \times \frac{2}{5}$$

Step 3
Simplify using the greatest common factor (GCF) if possible. Then multiply the numerators and denominators.

 $$\frac{^4\cancel{20}}{3} \times \frac{2}{\cancel{5}_1} = \frac{8}{3}$$

Step 4
Write the answer in simplest form.

$$\frac{8}{3} = 2\frac{2}{3}$$

Target These!

1. $6\frac{2}{3} \div 2\frac{1}{2} =$

2. $4\frac{2}{7} \div 2\frac{1}{2} =$

3. $1\frac{1}{6} \div 5\frac{1}{4} =$

4. $3\frac{1}{4} \div 2\frac{1}{6} =$

5. $2\frac{1}{2} \div 1\frac{1}{4} =$

6. $1\frac{1}{2} \div 6\frac{1}{2} =$

7. $3\frac{1}{4} \div 1\frac{3}{8} =$

8. $2\frac{3}{4} \div 1\frac{1}{3} =$

9. $1\frac{7}{8} \div 2\frac{1}{2} =$

10. $4\frac{1}{6} \div 2\frac{1}{3} =$

Answers: $2\frac{2}{3}$, $1\frac{5}{7}$, $\frac{2}{9}$, $1\frac{1}{2}$, 2, $\frac{3}{13}$, $2\frac{4}{11}$, $2\frac{1}{16}$, $\frac{3}{4}$, $1\frac{11}{14}$

Try using these four steps!

If your child is quick to solve the remaining math problems correctly, an occasional review may be all he or she needs. But if several of the answers are incorrect, it's a good idea to spend some time each day having your child work through a problem or two at home until he or she has mastered this skill.

Checkup 14

Name _____   Date _____

A. $6\frac{1}{4} \div 1\frac{1}{2} =$ $15\frac{1}{8} \div 5\frac{1}{2} =$ $2\frac{1}{4} \div 3\frac{3}{8} =$

B. $11\frac{1}{4} \div 3\frac{3}{8} =$ $6\frac{1}{4} \div 1\frac{1}{2} =$ $1\frac{3}{5} \div 3\frac{1}{5} =$

C. $8\frac{1}{2} \div 3\frac{7}{9} =$ $9\frac{3}{4} \div 3\frac{1}{4} =$

D. $1\frac{1}{5} \div 5\frac{2}{3} =$ $1\frac{1}{5} \div 3\frac{1}{3} =$

Test A: Dividing mixed numbers

©The Education Center, Inc. • *Target Math Success* • TEC60833 • Key p. 136

Checkup 14

Name _____   Date _____

A. $6\frac{1}{2} \div 1\frac{1}{2} =$ $6\frac{1}{2} \div 2\frac{1}{6} =$ $6\frac{2}{3} \div 1\frac{1}{9} =$

B. $3\frac{3}{7} \div 1\frac{1}{3} =$ $6\frac{2}{3} \div 2\frac{1}{2} =$ $3\frac{1}{2} \div 1\frac{3}{5} =$

C. $2\frac{2}{3} \div 6\frac{1}{2} =$ $2\frac{1}{5} \div 1\frac{3}{4} =$

D. $1\frac{1}{5} \div 1\frac{3}{5} =$ $2\frac{1}{4} \div 1\frac{7}{8} =$

Test B: Dividing mixed numbers

©The Education Center, Inc. • *Target Math Success* • TEC60833 • Key p. 136

Student Progress Chart

_____ (student)		Date	Number Correct	Comments
Checkup 1: Equivalent fractions	A			
Simplest form	B			
Checkup 2: Adding fractions with like denominators	A			
Subtracting fractions with like denominators	B			
Checkup 3: Adding fractions with unlike denominators	A			
Subtracting fractions with unlike denominators	B			
Checkup 4: Adding mixed numbers with like and unlike denominators	A			
Subtracting mixed numbers with like and unlike denominators	B			
Checkup 5: Subtracting mixed numbers with like and unlike denominators with regrouping	A			
	B			
Checkup 6: Subtracting fractions from whole numbers	A			
Subtracting fractions from mixed numbers	B			
Checkup 7: Multiplying fractions by fractions	A			
	B			

Student Progress Chart

_____ (student)		Date	Number Correct	Comments
Checkup 8: Multiplying fractions by whole numbers	A			
	B			
Checkup 9: Multiplying fractions by mixed numbers	A			
	B			
Checkup 10: Multiplying mixed numbers	A			
	B			
Checkup 11: Dividing a whole number by a fraction	A			
	B			
Checkup 12: Dividing a fraction by a whole number	A			
	B			
Checkup 13: Dividing a fraction by a fraction	A			
	B			
Checkup 14: Dividing mixed numbers	A			
	B			

Sweet Dreams!

Name _____ Date _____

Write the fraction shown.
Cross off the matching answer on the bear's blanket.
Some answers will not be crossed off.

Ant Farm?

Name _____ Date _____

Order each set of fractions from least to greatest.
Show your work on another sheet of paper.
Color if correct to show the path to the two workers.

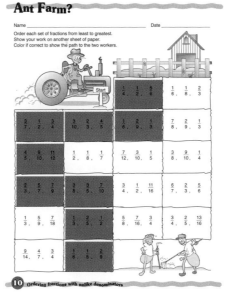

Bear Hair

Name _____ Date _____

Circle the correct set of factors for each number.
Write the greatest common factor for each pair of numbers in the box.

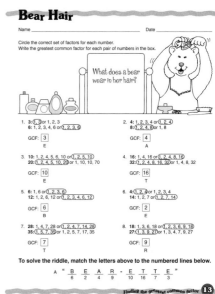

What does a bear wear in her hair?

1. 3: 1, 3 or 1, 2, 3
   6: 1, 2, 3, 4, 6 or 1, 2, 3, 6
   GCF: 3   I

2. 4: 1, 2, 3, 4 or 1, 2, 4
   8: 1, 2, 4, 8 or 1, 8
   GCF: 4   A

3. 10: 1, 2, 4, 5, 6, 10 or 1, 2, 5, 10
   20: 1, 2, 4, 5, 10, 20 or 1, 10, 10, 70
   GCF: 10   E

4. 16: 1, 4, 16 or 1, 2, 4, 8, 16
   32: 1, 2, 4, 8, 16, 32 or 1, 4, 8, 32
   GCF: 16   T

5. 6: 1, 6 or 1, 2, 3, 6
   12: 1, 2, 6, 12 or 1, 2, 3, 4, 6, 12
   GCF: 6   B

6. 4: 1, 4 or 1, 2, 3, 4
   14: 1, 2, 7 or 1, 2, 7, 14
   GCF: 2   E

7. 28: 1, 4, 7, 28 or 1, 2, 4, 7, 14, 28
   35: 1, 5, 7, 35 or 1, 2, 5, 7, 17, 35
   GCF: 7   R

8. 18: 1, 3, 6, 18 or 1, 2, 3, 6, 9, 18
   27: 1, 3, 9, 27 or 1, 3, 4, 7, 9, 27
   GCF: 9   D

To solve the riddle, match the letters above to the numbered lines below.

A " B E A R - E T T E "
    6 2 4 9   10 16 7 3

Saturn's Rings?

Name _____ Date _____

Compare the fractions.
Write <, >, or =.
Color by the code.

Color Code
< = orange
> = yellow
= = red

Which Pizza?

Name _____ Date _____

Find the least common multiple.
Color to show the path to the pizza.

3 and 4	12	8	6	16
2 and 5	5	10	15	4
7 and 9	16	56	63	126
3 and 8	8	12	24	16
2 and 4	2	8	6	4
3 and 9	27	18	9	6
4 and 5	15	20	40	30
2 and 6	3	6	12	16
9 and 4	36	24	40	13
12 and 3	4	12	36	15
6 and 8	48	36	24	32
2 and 7	7	24	21	14
6 and 10	10	60	16	30
8 and 5	20	45	40	50
3 and 6	3	6	9	18
5 and 7	35	30	12	45
8 and 12	24	12	6	45
4 and 6	24	12	36	48

mushrooms   papaya   peppers   pineapple

Sneaking Some Snacks

Name _____ Date _____

Match each fraction to its simplest form.
Color each pair of equivalent fractions the same color.

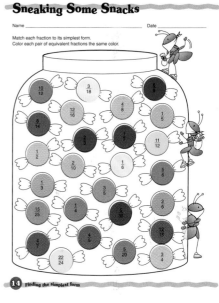

Extra Sharp Cheese

Name _____ Date _____

Order each set of fractions from least to greatest.
To answer the riddle, write the letter of the corresponding fraction in each box.
The first one has been done for you.

When does a piece of cheese become an artist?

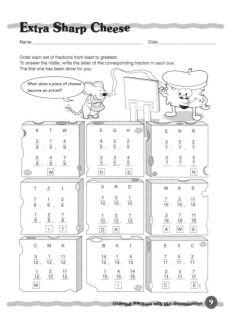

H₂O Humor

Name _____ Date _____

Circle the equivalent fraction.
To solve the riddle, match the letter to the
equivalent fraction on the right.
The first one has been done for you.

WHEN IT
REACHES
THE
BOTTOM

Power Practice

Name _____ Date _____

Write each fraction in simplest form.

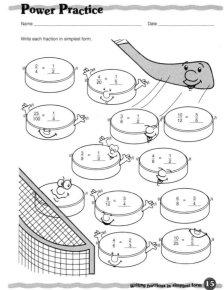

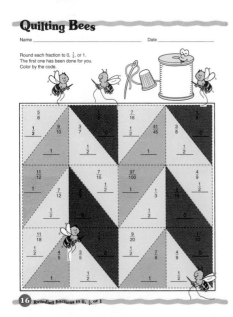

Quilting Bees

Name _____ Date _____

Round each fraction to 0, $\frac{1}{2}$, or 1.
The first one has been done for you.
Color by the code.

16 Rounding fractions to 0, $\frac{1}{2}$, or 1

Up, Up, and Away!

Name _____ Date _____

Add.
Cross off the matching answer on the hot-air balloon basket.
Some answers will not be crossed off.

Adding fractions with like denominators 21

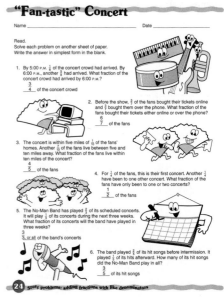

"Fan-tastic" Concert

Name _____ Date _____

Read.
Solve each problem on another sheet of paper.
Write the answer in simplest form in the blank.

1. By 5:00 P.M. $\frac{1}{8}$ of the concert crowd had arrived. By 6:00 P.M., another $\frac{5}{8}$ had arrived. What fraction of the concert crowd had arrived by 6:00 P.M.?
   $\frac{3}{4}$ of the concert crowd

2. Before the show, $\frac{3}{7}$ of the fans bought their tickets online and $\frac{3}{7}$ bought them over the phone. What fraction of the fans bought their tickets either online or over the phone?
   $\frac{6}{7}$ of the fans

3. The concert is within five miles of $\frac{1}{5}$ of the fans' homes. Another $\frac{3}{5}$ of the fans live between five and ten miles away. What fraction of the fans live within ten miles of the concert?
   $\frac{4}{5}$ of the fans

4. For $\frac{1}{4}$ of the fans, this is their first concert. Another $\frac{1}{4}$ have been to one other concert. What fraction of the fans have only been to one or two concerts?
   $\frac{1}{2}$ of the fans

5. The No-Man Band has played $\frac{2}{3}$ of its scheduled concerts. It will play $\frac{1}{3}$ of its concerts during the next three weeks. What fraction of its concerts will the band have played in three weeks?
   $\frac{3}{3}$, or all of the band's concerts

6. The band played $\frac{2}{5}$ of its hit songs before intermission. It played $\frac{1}{5}$ of its hits afterward. How many of its hit songs did the No-Man Band play in all?
   $\frac{3}{5}$ of its hit songs

24 Story Problems: adding fractions with like denominators

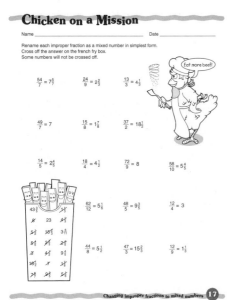

Chicken on a Mission

Name _____ Date _____

Rename each improper fraction as a mixed number in simplest form.
Cross off the answer on the french fry box.
Some numbers will not be crossed off.

17 Changing improper fractions to mixed numbers

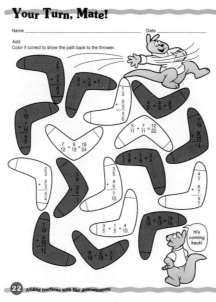

Your Turn, Mate!

Name _____ Date _____

Add.
Color if correct to show the path back to the thrower.

22 Adding fractions with like denominators

Polar Beach

Name _____ Date _____

Add.
Show your work.
Write the answer in simplest form.
Cross off the answer on the lifeguard chair.
Some numbers will not be crossed off.

25 Adding fractions with unlike denominators

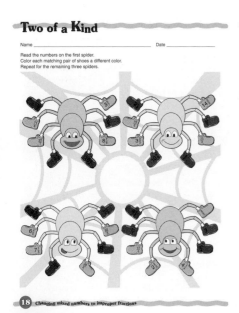

Two of a Kind

Name _____ Date _____

Read the numbers on the first spider.
Color each matching pair of shoes a different color.
Repeat for the remaining three spiders.

18 Changing mixed numbers to improper fractions

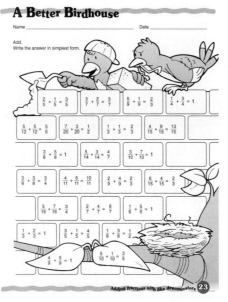

A Better Birdhouse

Name _____ Date _____

Add.
Write the answer in simplest form.

23 Adding fractions with like denominators

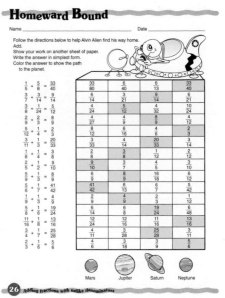

Homeward Bound

Name _____ Date _____

Follow the directions below to help Alvin Alien find his way home.
Add.
Show your work on another sheet of paper.
Write the answer in simplest form.
Color the answer to show the path to the planet.

Mars   Jupiter   Saturn   Neptune

26 Adding fractions with unlike denominators

Dance Party DJ

Name _____ Date _____

Add.
Show your work.
Write in simplest form.

$\frac{1}{8} + \frac{1}{9} = \frac{17}{72}$

$+ \frac{2}{?} \quad \frac{13}{15}$

$\frac{1}{4} + \frac{5}{8} = \frac{7}{8}$

$\frac{1}{3} + \frac{?}{?} \quad \frac{17}{24}$

$\frac{4}{5} + \frac{1}{9} \quad \frac{41}{45}$

$\frac{2}{7} + \frac{1}{5} = \frac{17}{35}$

$\frac{1}{2} + \frac{5}{11} \quad \frac{21}{22}$

$\frac{5}{6} + \frac{1}{18} = \frac{8}{9}$

$\frac{1}{10} + \frac{3}{4} \quad \frac{17}{20}$

$\frac{7}{8} + \frac{1}{16} = \frac{15}{16}$

$\frac{1}{4} + \frac{1}{3} = \frac{7}{12}$

$\frac{1}{2} + \frac{1}{3} \quad \frac{5}{6}$

$\frac{3}{4} + \frac{1}{12} = \frac{5}{6}$

$\frac{6}{7} + \frac{1}{8} \quad \frac{55}{56}$

$\frac{1}{4} + \frac{5}{16} \quad \frac{9}{16}$

$\frac{3}{4} + \frac{1}{6} = \frac{11}{12}$

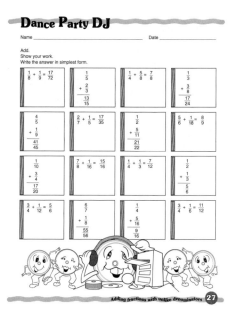

Adding fractions with unlike denominators **27**

Hold On!

Name _____ Date _____

Add.
Show your work on another sheet of paper.
Color if correct.

$1\frac{1}{10} + 4\frac{6}{10} = 5\frac{7}{10}$

$5\frac{1}{4} + 1\frac{3}{9} = 6\frac{7}{12}$

$3\frac{5}{8} + 5\frac{3}{4} = 9\frac{3}{8}$

$2\frac{1}{3} + 6\frac{9}{9} = 9\frac{1}{3}$

$6\frac{3}{10} + 7\frac{7}{10} = 15$

$7\frac{3}{8} + 5\frac{1}{2} = 13\frac{1}{2}$

$4\frac{4}{7} + 6\frac{13}{14} = 11\frac{11}{14}$

$8\frac{2}{3} + 1\frac{6}{9} = 10\frac{4}{9}$

$11\frac{5}{6} + 3\frac{1}{18} = 14\frac{8}{9}$

$5\frac{5}{9} + 8\frac{5}{18} = 15\frac{4}{9}$

$20\frac{4}{7} + 9\frac{5}{14} = 29\frac{9}{14}$

$9\frac{3}{4} + 2\frac{5}{16} = 12$

$15\frac{3}{4} + 2\frac{3}{8} = 15\frac{17}{24}$

$10\frac{7}{8} + 4\frac{5}{9} = 15\frac{1}{6}$

$4\frac{2}{9} + 1\frac{4}{18} = 6\frac{1}{9}$

$12\frac{3}{4} + 5\frac{1}{4} = 18$

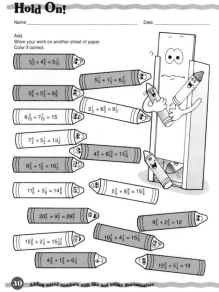

30 *Adding mixed numbers with like and unlike denominators*

Flower Power

Name _____ Date _____

Subtract.
Show your work.
Color the flower with the matching answer.
Some flowers will not be colored.

$\frac{7}{11} - \frac{3}{11} = \frac{4}{11}$

$\frac{2}{3} - \frac{1}{3} = \frac{1}{3}$

$\frac{4}{5} - \frac{2}{5} = \frac{2}{5}$

$\frac{8}{17} - \frac{7}{17} = \frac{1}{17}$

$\frac{10}{21} - \frac{8}{21} = \frac{2}{21}$

$\frac{3}{5} - \frac{2}{5} = \frac{1}{5}$

$\frac{5}{6} - \frac{2}{6} = \frac{6}{7}$

$\frac{14}{15} - \frac{13}{15} = \frac{17}{19} - \frac{5}{19} = \frac{15}{23} - \frac{10}{23} = \frac{5}{7} - \frac{2}{7}$

$\frac{8}{9} - \frac{4}{9} = \frac{10}{11} - \frac{6}{11} = \frac{6}{7} - \frac{5}{7} = \frac{13}{15} - \frac{2}{15}$

$\frac{11}{13} - \frac{6}{13} = \frac{23}{35} - \frac{11}{35} = \frac{5}{13} - \frac{12}{13}$

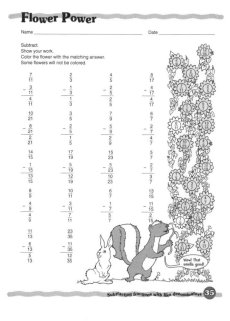

Wow! That smells good!

Subtraction fractions with like denominators **35**

Longing for a Goal

Name _____ Date _____

Read.
Show your work on another sheet of paper.
Write the answer in simplest form in the blank.

1. On the Spotstown soccer team, $\frac{1}{4}$ of the players are 9 years old, and $\frac{1}{5}$ of the players are 10 years old. What fraction of the team's players are either 9 or 10 years old? ____ of the team

2. During practice today, $\frac{3}{8}$ of the team practiced dribbling while $\frac{1}{5}$ of the team practiced penalty kicks. What fraction of the team practiced dribbling or penalty kicks? ____ of the team

3. At Wednesday's game, $\frac{1}{7}$ of the team scored a goal. During Thursday's game, $\frac{1}{3}$ of the team scored a goal. What fraction of the team scored a goal during Wednesday's or Thursday's games? ____ of the team

4. During the season, $\frac{1}{12}$ of the games and $\frac{1}{4}$ of the practices were canceled for rain. What fraction of the games and practices were canceled for rain? ____ of the games and practices

5. On the team, $\frac{3}{8}$ of the players can play forward, and $\frac{1}{6}$ of the players can play goalie. What fraction of players can play forward or goalie? ____ of the players

6. The team tied $\frac{1}{6}$ of their games and lost $\frac{1}{9}$ of their games. What fraction of the games did the team lose or tie? ____ of the games

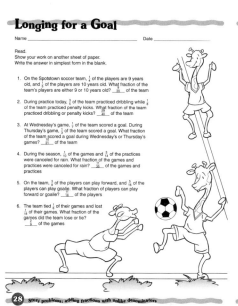

28 *Story problems: adding fractions with unlike denominators*

Sweet Tooth

Name _____ Date _____

Add.
Show your work.
Color the matching answer.
Some jelly beans will not be colored.

$7\frac{3}{8} + 4\frac{2}{5} = 11\frac{31}{40}$

$4\frac{2}{3} + 2\frac{1}{7} = 6\frac{16}{21}$

$3\frac{1}{4} + 8\frac{3}{4} = 12$

$1\frac{1}{2} + 3\frac{5}{6} = 5\frac{1}{6}$

$5\frac{3}{4} + 1\frac{9}{10} = 7\frac{7}{40}$

$5\frac{7}{10} + 6\frac{4}{5} = 12\frac{1}{2}$

$6\frac{4}{7} + 7\frac{5}{6} = 14\frac{3}{7}$

$5\frac{3}{4} + 9\frac{1}{2} = 15\frac{1}{4}$

$9\frac{5}{6} + 2\frac{2}{3} = 12\frac{1}{2}$

$8\frac{1}{2} + 5\frac{5}{6} = 14\frac{1}{3}$

$3\frac{3}{4} + 1\frac{7}{8} = 5\frac{5}{8}$

$4\frac{1}{4} + 1\frac{5}{6} = 5\frac{11}{12}$

$9\frac{3}{5} + 7\frac{1}{5} = 16\frac{4}{5}$

$6\frac{3}{8} + 2\frac{5}{6} = 9\frac{5}{24}$

$8\frac{1}{3} + 1\frac{5}{9} = 9\frac{8}{9}$

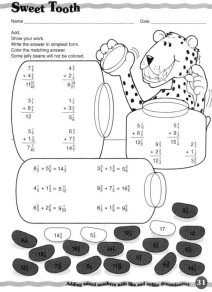

Adding mixed numbers with like and unlike denominators **31**

House-Hunting Hermie

Name _____ Date _____

Subtract.
Show your work on another sheet of paper.
Write the answer in simplest form.
Color if correct.
Connect the colored boxes to show the path to the shell.

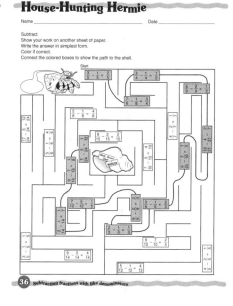

36 *Subtracting fractions with like denominators*

"Mane" Attraction

Name _____ Date _____

Add.
Show your work.
Write the answer in simplest form.

$2\frac{1}{4} + 4\frac{1}{4} = 6\frac{1}{2}$ = A

$3\frac{5}{8} + 6\frac{1}{8} = 9\frac{3}{4}$ = E

$5\frac{5}{8} + 8\frac{3}{8} = 14$ = R

$1\frac{1}{8} + 9\frac{3}{8} = 10\frac{1}{2}$ = T

$7\frac{7}{8} + 3\frac{1}{8} = 11\frac{1}{2}$ = E

$8\frac{5}{10} + 3\frac{1}{10} = 11\frac{3}{5}$ = E

$2\frac{1}{4} + 6\frac{1}{4} = 8\frac{1}{2}$ = O

$4\frac{1}{3} + 1\frac{2}{3} = 6\frac{1}{3}$ = N

$9\frac{1}{2} + 7\frac{1}{2} = 17$ = A

$6\frac{3}{4} + 5\frac{3}{4} = 12\frac{1}{2}$ = A

$4\frac{1}{5} + 9\frac{4}{5} = 11$ = G

$2\frac{3}{5} + 4\frac{4}{5} = 7\frac{2}{5}$ = P

$5\frac{1}{2} + 5\frac{1}{2} = 8\frac{3}{4}$ = E

$7\frac{5}{6} + 8\frac{1}{6} = 16$ = T

$2\frac{3}{4} + 2\frac{3}{4} = 5\frac{1}{4}$ = A

$4\frac{1}{5} + 9\frac{4}{5} = 11$ = I

What's another name for hair?

To answer the question on the mirror, match the letters above to the numbered lines below.

E A R - T O - E A R   C A R P E T I N G
$8\frac{1}{2}$ $6\frac{1}{2}$ $6\frac{1}{3}$ $10\frac{1}{2}$ 17 $11\frac{1}{2}$ $12\frac{1}{2}$ $5\frac{1}{2}$ $5\frac{1}{4}$ 14 $7\frac{2}{5}$ $11\frac{3}{5}$ 16 11 11

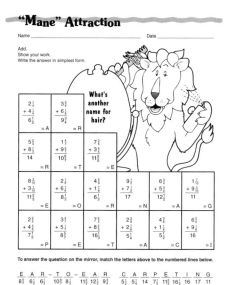

Adding mixed numbers with like denominators **29**

Bake Sale Goodies

Name _____ Date _____

Read.
Show your work on another sheet of paper.
Write the answer in simplest form in the blank provided.

Follow me to the bake sale!

1. Becky is making brownies for the bake sale. The recipe calls for $1\frac{1}{2}$ cups of walnuts and $1\frac{1}{4}$ cups of pecans. How many total cups of nuts will Becky need for the cake? _$2\frac{3}{4}$_ cups

2. Chris will make his favorite peanut butter cookies. He has already added $2\frac{1}{4}$ cups of flour and $1\frac{1}{3}$ cups of sugar. How much flour and sugar has Chris added all together? _$3\frac{5}{12}$_ cups

3. To make his grandmother's best rolls, Hal needs $2\frac{1}{2}$ teaspoons of dry yeast and $1\frac{1}{2}$ teaspoons of salt. How much salt and yeast does Hal need? _4_ teaspoons

4. The roll dough has to rise for $2\frac{1}{2}$ hours. After Hal shapes the rolls, they need to rise for $1\frac{1}{2}$ hours more. How many total hours does the roll dough need to rise? _4_ hours

5. Hal has $3\frac{1}{4}$ dozen rolls for the bake sale. Dan brought $1\frac{1}{2}$ dozen cookies for the sale. How many dozens of treats do Hal and Dan have in all for the bake sale? _$4\frac{3}{4}$_ dozens

6. Anna is baking $1\frac{5}{6}$ dozen cupcakes. She is also making $2\frac{1}{2}$ dozen popcorn balls. How many dozens of treats is Anna bringing to the bake sale? _$4\frac{1}{3}$_ dozens

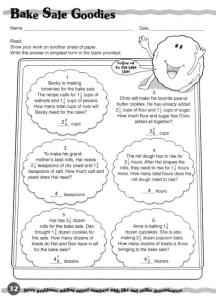

32 *Story problems: adding mixed numbers with like and unlike denominators*

On the Beach

Name _____ Date _____

Subtract.
Show your work.
Write the answer in simplest form.
Color by the code.

Color Code
$\frac{1}{2}$ = blue $\frac{1}{5}$ = green
$\frac{1}{3}$ = purple $\frac{1}{6}$ = orange
$\frac{1}{4}$ = brown $\frac{1}{7}$ = yellow

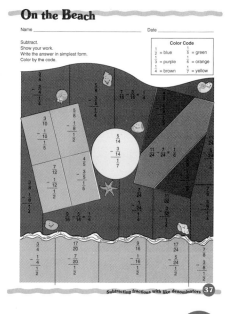

Subtracting fractions with like denominators **37**

129

Picture-Perfect

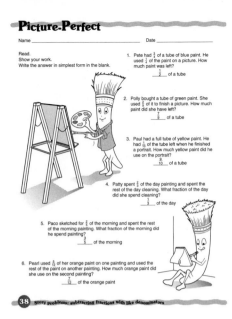

Name ______________________ Date ______________

Read.
Show your work.
Write the answer in simplest form in the blank.

1. Pete had $\frac{3}{4}$ of a tube of blue paint. He used $\frac{1}{4}$ of the paint on a picture. How much paint was left? $\frac{1}{2}$ of a tube

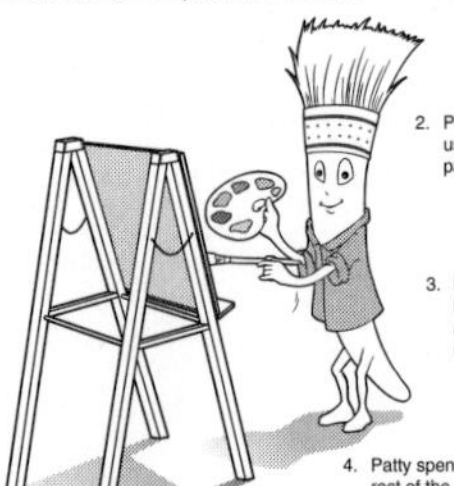

2. Polly bought a tube of green paint. She used $\frac{2}{9}$ of it to finish a picture. How much paint did she have left? $\frac{7}{9}$ of a tube

3. Paul had a full tube of yellow paint. He had $\frac{1}{10}$ of the tube left when he finished a portrait. How much yellow paint did he use on the portrait? $\frac{9}{10}$ of a tube

4. Patty spent $\frac{2}{3}$ of the day painting and spent the rest of the day cleaning. What fraction of the day did she spend cleaning? $\frac{1}{3}$ of the day

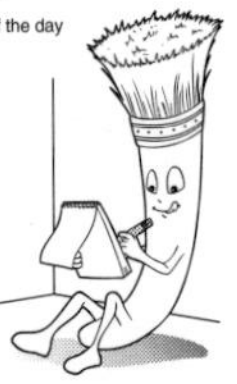

5. Paco sketched for $\frac{2}{5}$ of the morning and spent the rest of the morning painting. What fraction of the morning did he spend painting? $\frac{3}{5}$ of the morning

6. Pearl used $\frac{5}{12}$ of her orange paint on one painting and used the rest of the paint on another painting. How much orange paint did she use on the second painting? $\frac{7}{12}$ of the orange paint

38 Story problems: subtracting fractions with like denominators

Alley-Oop!

Name ______________________ Date ______________

Subtract.
Show your work.
Write the answer in simplest form.

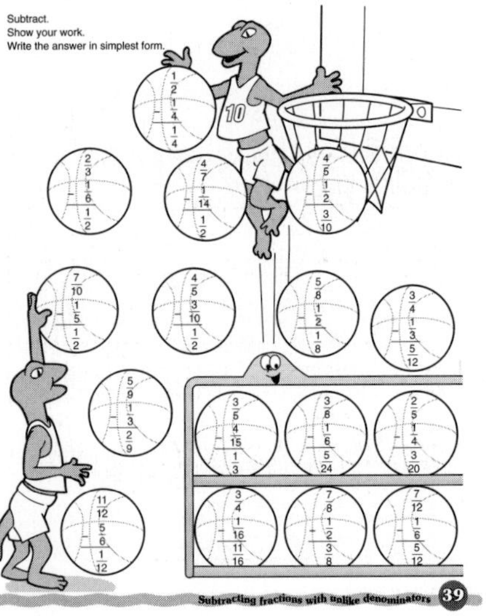

10
$\frac{1}{2} - \frac{1}{4} = \frac{1}{4}$
$\frac{2}{3} - \frac{1}{6} = \frac{1}{2}$
$\frac{4}{7} - \frac{1}{14} = \frac{1}{2}$
$\frac{4}{5} - \frac{1}{2} = \frac{3}{10}$
$\frac{7}{10} - \frac{1}{5} = \frac{1}{2}$
$\frac{4}{5} - \frac{3}{10} = \frac{1}{2}$
$\frac{5}{8} - \frac{1}{2} = \frac{1}{8}$
$\frac{3}{4} - \frac{1}{3} = \frac{5}{12}$
$\frac{5}{9} - \frac{1}{3} = \frac{2}{9}$
$\frac{3}{5} - \frac{4}{15} = \frac{1}{3}$
$\frac{3}{8} - \frac{1}{6} = \frac{5}{24}$
$\frac{2}{5} - \frac{1}{4} = \frac{3}{20}$
$\frac{11}{12} - \frac{5}{6} = \frac{1}{12}$
$\frac{3}{4} - \frac{1}{16} = \frac{11}{16}$
$\frac{7}{8} - \frac{1}{2} = \frac{3}{8}$
$\frac{7}{12} - \frac{1}{6} = \frac{5}{12}$

Subtracting fractions with unlike denominators 39

New Moon's Mission

Name ______________________ Date ______________

Subtract.
Show your work.
Write the answer in simplest form.

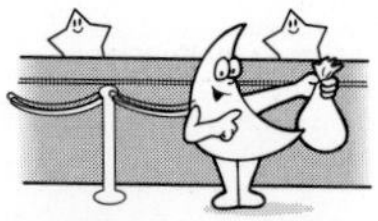

Why did the moon go to the bank?

$\frac{2}{3} - \frac{1}{5} = \frac{7}{15}$ | $\frac{3}{4} - \frac{2}{3} = \frac{1}{12}$

$\frac{5}{8} - \frac{1}{3} = \frac{7}{24}$ | $\frac{5}{6} - \frac{5}{12} = \frac{5}{12}$

$\frac{7}{8} - \frac{3}{4} = \frac{1}{8}$ | $\frac{4}{9} - \frac{1}{3} = \frac{1}{9}$ | $\frac{9}{10} - \frac{4}{5} = \frac{1}{10}$

$\frac{5}{12} - \frac{3}{8} = \frac{1}{24}$ | $\frac{3}{5} - \frac{7}{15} = \frac{2}{15}$ | $\frac{4}{7} - \frac{1}{3} = \frac{5}{21}$

$\frac{1}{2} - \frac{1}{8} = \frac{3}{8}$ | $\frac{4}{5} - \frac{3}{8} = \frac{17}{40}$ | $\frac{1}{4} - \frac{1}{6} = \frac{1}{12}$

$\frac{1}{2} - \frac{1}{3} = \frac{1}{6}$ | $\frac{6}{7} - \frac{1}{2} = \frac{5}{14}$ | $\frac{8}{9} - \frac{2}{3} = \frac{2}{9}$

To answer the riddle, color the letter below that contains each correct answer.

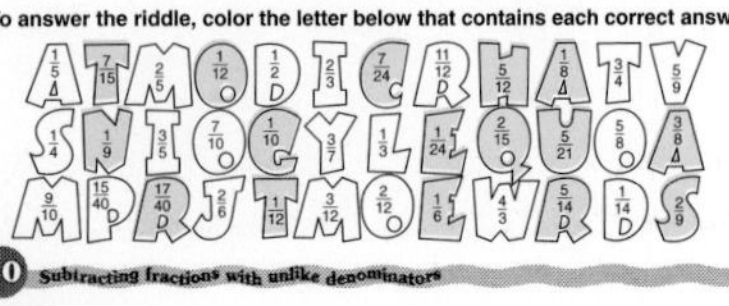

A T M O D I C R H A T Y
S N I O G Y L E Q U O A
M P R J T M O E W R D S

40 Subtracting fractions with unlike denominators

Macaroni and Cheese, Please!

Name ______________________ Date ______________

Subtract.
Show your work on another sheet of paper.
Color if correct.

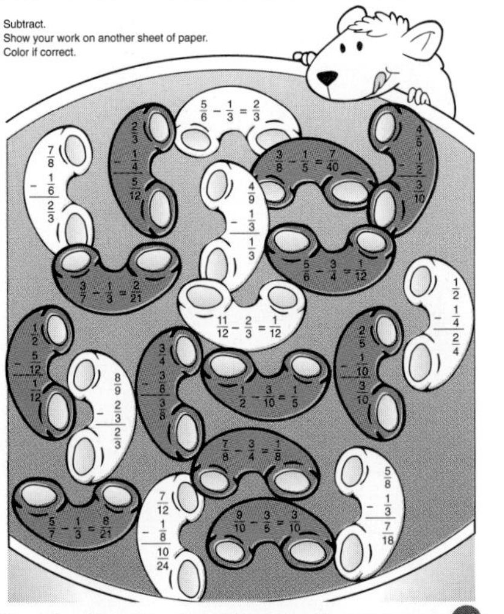

$\frac{5}{6} - \frac{1}{3} = \frac{2}{3}$
$\frac{7}{8} - \frac{1}{6} = \frac{2}{3}$
$\frac{2}{3} - \frac{1}{4} = \frac{5}{12}$
$\frac{3}{8} - \frac{1}{5} = \frac{7}{40}$
$\frac{4}{5} - \frac{1}{2} = \frac{3}{10}$
$\frac{4}{9} - \frac{1}{3} = \frac{1}{3}$
$\frac{5}{6} - \frac{3}{4} = \frac{1}{12}$
$\frac{3}{7} - \frac{1}{3} = \frac{2}{21}$
$\frac{11}{12} - \frac{2}{3} = \frac{1}{12}$
$\frac{1}{2} - \frac{1}{4} = \frac{2}{4}$
$\frac{1}{2} - \frac{5}{12} = \frac{1}{12}$
$\frac{8}{9} - \frac{2}{3} = \frac{2}{3}$
$\frac{3}{4} - \frac{3}{8} = \frac{3}{8}$
$\frac{1}{2} - \frac{3}{10} = \frac{1}{5}$
$\frac{2}{5} - \frac{1}{10} = \frac{3}{10}$
$\frac{7}{8} - \frac{3}{4} = \frac{1}{8}$
$\frac{5}{7} - \frac{1}{3} = \frac{8}{21}$
$\frac{7}{12} - \frac{1}{8} = \frac{10}{24}$
$\frac{9}{10} - \frac{3}{5} = \frac{3}{10}$
$\frac{5}{8} - \frac{1}{3} = \frac{7}{18}$

Subtracting fractions with unlike denominators 41

"Stud-ant" Field Trip

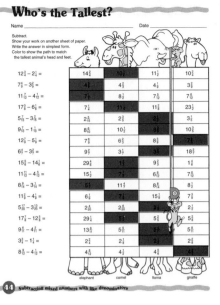

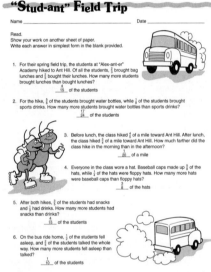

Name ______________________ Date ______________

Read.
Show your work on another sheet of paper.
Write each answer in simplest form in the blank provided.

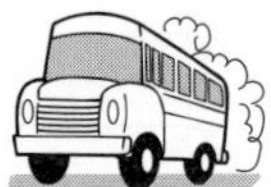

1. For their spring field trip, the students at "Alex-ant-er" Academy hiked to Ant Hill. Of all the students, $\frac{2}{3}$ brought bag lunches and $\frac{2}{5}$ bought their lunches. How many more students brought lunches than bought lunches? $\frac{4}{15}$ of the students

2. For the hike, $\frac{5}{6}$ of the students brought water bottles, while $\frac{1}{8}$ of the students brought sports drinks. How many more students brought water bottles than sports drinks? $\frac{17}{24}$ of the students

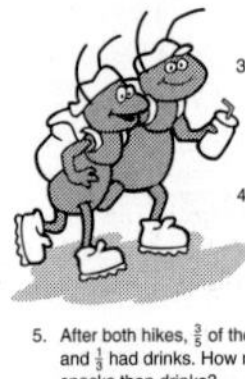

3. Before lunch, the class hiked $\frac{4}{5}$ of a mile toward Ant Hill. After lunch, the class hiked $\frac{3}{4}$ of a mile toward Ant Hill. How much farther did the class hike in the morning than in the afternoon? $\frac{1}{20}$ of a mile

4. Everyone in the class wore a hat. Baseball caps made up $\frac{5}{8}$ of the hats, while $\frac{1}{4}$ of the hats were floppy hats. How many more hats were baseball caps than floppy hats? $\frac{3}{8}$ of the hats

5. After both hikes, $\frac{3}{5}$ of the students had snacks and $\frac{1}{3}$ had drinks. How many more students had snacks than drinks? $\frac{4}{15}$ of the students

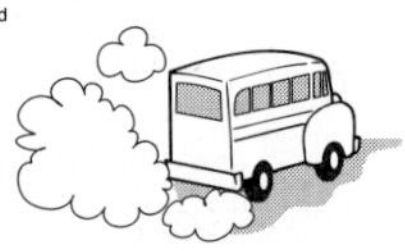

6. On the bus ride home, $\frac{1}{2}$ of the students fell asleep, and $\frac{2}{5}$ of the students talked the whole way. How many more students fell asleep than talked? $\frac{1}{10}$ of the students

42 Story problems: subtracting fractions with unlike denominators

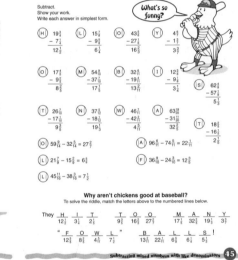

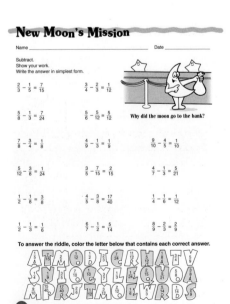

It's in the Mail!

Name ______________________ Date ______________

Subtract.
Show your work.
Write the answer in simplest form.
Cross off the answer on the mailbox.
Some numbers will not be crossed off.

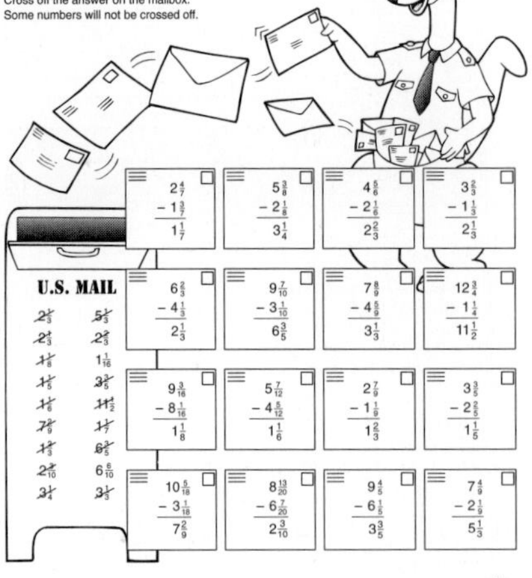

$2\frac{4}{7} - 1\frac{3}{7} = 1\frac{1}{7}$
$5\frac{3}{8} - 2\frac{1}{8} = 3\frac{1}{4}$
$4\frac{5}{6} - 2\frac{1}{6} = 2\frac{2}{3}$
$3\frac{2}{3} - 1\frac{1}{3} = 2\frac{1}{3}$
U.S. MAIL
$2\frac{1}{3}$ $5\frac{1}{3}$ $2\frac{1}{3}$ $2\frac{2}{3}$ $1\frac{1}{8}$ $1\frac{1}{16}$ $1\frac{1}{5}$ $3\frac{3}{5}$ $1\frac{1}{6}$ $11\frac{1}{2}$ $7\frac{2}{9}$ $1\frac{1}{7}$ $1\frac{2}{3}$ $6\frac{3}{5}$ $2\frac{3}{10}$ $6\frac{6}{10}$ $3\frac{1}{4}$ $3\frac{1}{3}$
$6\frac{2}{3} - 4\frac{1}{3} = 2\frac{1}{3}$
$9\frac{7}{10} - 3\frac{1}{10} = 6\frac{3}{5}$
$7\frac{8}{9} - 4\frac{5}{9} = 3\frac{1}{3}$
$12\frac{3}{4} - 1\frac{1}{4} = 11\frac{1}{2}$
$9\frac{3}{16} - 8\frac{1}{16} = 1\frac{1}{8}$
$5\frac{7}{12} - 4\frac{5}{12} = 1\frac{1}{6}$
$2\frac{7}{9} - 1\frac{1}{9} = 1\frac{2}{3}$
$3\frac{3}{5} - 2\frac{2}{5} = 1\frac{1}{5}$
$10\frac{5}{18} - 3\frac{1}{18} = 7\frac{2}{9}$
$8\frac{13}{20} - 6\frac{7}{20} = 2\frac{3}{10}$
$9\frac{4}{5} - 6\frac{1}{5} = 3\frac{3}{5}$
$7\frac{4}{9} - 2\frac{1}{9} = 5\frac{1}{3}$

Subtracting mixed numbers with like denominators 43

Who's the Tallest?

Name ______________________ Date ______________

Subtract.
Show your work on another sheet of paper.
Write the answer in simplest form.
Color to show the path to match the tallest animal's head and feet.

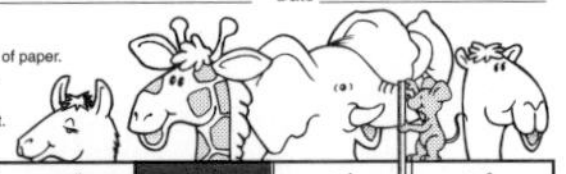

$12\frac{3}{4} - 2\frac{1}{4} =$	$14\frac{2}{4}$	$10\frac{1}{2}$	$11\frac{1}{2}$	$10\frac{2}{4}$
$7\frac{4}{9} - 3\frac{2}{9} =$	$4\frac{2}{9}$	$4\frac{2}{3}$	$4\frac{1}{9}$	$3\frac{2}{9}$
$11\frac{7}{12} - 4\frac{1}{12} =$	$7\frac{1}{2}$	$8\frac{1}{2}$	$7\frac{5}{12}$	$7\frac{6}{12}$
$17\frac{3}{8} - 6\frac{1}{8} =$	$7\frac{1}{4}$	$11\frac{1}{4}$	$11\frac{2}{8}$	$23\frac{1}{2}$
$5\frac{7}{15} - 3\frac{2}{15} =$	$2\frac{5}{15}$	$2\frac{3}{5}$	$2\frac{1}{3}$	$3\frac{1}{5}$
$9\frac{7}{10} - 1\frac{1}{10} =$	$8\frac{6}{10}$	$10\frac{1}{2}$	$8\frac{3}{5}$	$10\frac{3}{5}$
$12\frac{7}{9} - 5\frac{1}{9} =$	$7\frac{6}{9}$	$6\frac{2}{3}$	$8\frac{5}{9}$	$7\frac{2}{3}$
$6\frac{4}{7} - 3\frac{2}{7} =$	$9\frac{2}{7}$	$3\frac{1}{7}$	$3\frac{2}{7}$	$18\frac{2}{7}$
$15\frac{5}{6} - 14\frac{1}{6} =$	$29\frac{4}{6}$	$1\frac{2}{3}$	$9\frac{2}{3}$	$1\frac{4}{6}$
$11\frac{11}{12} - 4\frac{5}{12} =$	$15\frac{1}{2}$	$7\frac{1}{2}$	$6\frac{6}{12}$	$7\frac{6}{12}$
$8\frac{9}{14} - 3\frac{1}{14} =$	$5\frac{4}{7}$	$11\frac{4}{7}$	$8\frac{8}{14}$	$8\frac{1}{2}$
$11\frac{2}{9} - 4\frac{1}{9} =$	$6\frac{1}{9}$	$7\frac{1}{9}$	$15\frac{1}{9}$	$7\frac{3}{9}$
$5\frac{17}{20} - 3\frac{13}{20} =$	$2\frac{4}{20}$	$2\frac{6}{20}$	$2\frac{1}{5}$	$2\frac{1}{2}$
$17\frac{7}{8} - 12\frac{5}{8} =$	$29\frac{1}{4}$	$5\frac{1}{4}$	$5\frac{2}{5}$	$5\frac{2}{8}$
$9\frac{6}{11} - 4\frac{2}{11} =$	$13\frac{8}{11}$	$5\frac{5}{11}$	$5\frac{4}{11}$	$5\frac{8}{11}$
$3\frac{3}{4} - 1\frac{1}{4} =$	$2\frac{2}{4}$	$2\frac{1}{8}$	$2\frac{1}{2}$	$2\frac{2}{8}$
$8\frac{9}{12} - 4\frac{1}{12} =$	$4\frac{8}{12}$	$4\frac{1}{2}$	$4\frac{5}{6}$	$4\frac{2}{3}$

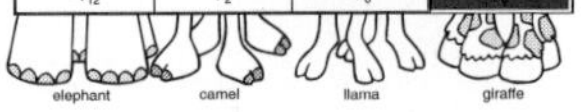

elephant
camel
llama
giraffe

44 Subtracting mixed numbers with like denominators

Hen Humor

Name ______________________ Date ______________

Subtract.
Show your work.
Write each answer in simplest form.

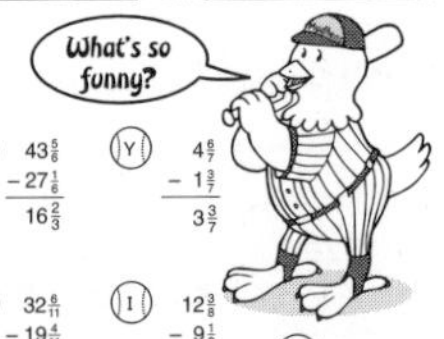

What's so funny?

(H) $19\frac{3}{4} - 7\frac{1}{4} = 12\frac{1}{2}$

(L) $15\frac{7}{8} - 9\frac{5}{8} = 6\frac{1}{4}$

(O) $43\frac{5}{6} - 27\frac{1}{6} = 16\frac{2}{3}$

(Y) $4\frac{6}{7} - 1\frac{3}{7} = 3\frac{3}{7}$

(O) $17\frac{4}{5} - 9\frac{2}{5} = 8\frac{2}{5}$

(M) $54\frac{9}{10} - 37\frac{7}{10} = 17\frac{1}{5}$

(B) $32\frac{6}{11} - 19\frac{4}{11} = 13\frac{2}{11}$

(I) $12\frac{3}{8} - 9\frac{1}{8} = 3\frac{1}{4}$

(S) $62\frac{4}{9} - 57\frac{1}{9} = 5\frac{1}{3}$

(T) $26\frac{7}{10} - 17\frac{1}{10} = 9\frac{3}{5}$

(N) $37\frac{5}{12} - 18\frac{1}{12} = 19\frac{1}{3}$

(W) $46\frac{7}{11} - 42\frac{2}{11} = 4\frac{5}{11}$

(A) $63\frac{19}{20} - 31\frac{11}{20} = 32\frac{2}{5}$

(T) $18\frac{2}{5} - 16\frac{1}{5} = 2\frac{1}{5}$

(O) $59\frac{9}{14} - 32\frac{5}{14} = 27\frac{2}{7}$

(A) $96\frac{6}{11} - 74\frac{5}{11} = 22\frac{1}{11}$

(L) $21\frac{7}{9} - 15\frac{2}{9} = 6\frac{5}{9}$

(F) $36\frac{9}{10} - 24\frac{3}{10} = 12\frac{3}{5}$

(L) $45\frac{11}{16} - 38\frac{3}{16} = 7\frac{1}{2}$

Why aren't chickens good at baseball?

To solve the riddle, match the letters above to the numbered lines below.

They H ($12\frac{1}{2}$) I ($3\frac{1}{4}$) T ($2\frac{1}{5}$)   T ($9\frac{3}{5}$) O ($16\frac{2}{3}$) O ($27\frac{2}{7}$)   M ($17\frac{1}{5}$) A ($32\frac{2}{5}$) N ($19\frac{1}{3}$) Y ($3\frac{3}{7}$)

"F ($12\frac{3}{5}$) O ($8\frac{2}{5}$) W ($4\frac{5}{11}$) L ($7\frac{1}{2}$)"   B ($13\frac{2}{11}$) A ($22\frac{1}{11}$) L ($6\frac{5}{9}$) L ($6\frac{1}{4}$) S ($5\frac{1}{3}$)!

Subtracting mixed numbers with like denominators 45

Cooking Class

Name ______________________ Date ______________

Read.
Show your work on another sheet of paper.
Write each answer in simplest form in the blank.

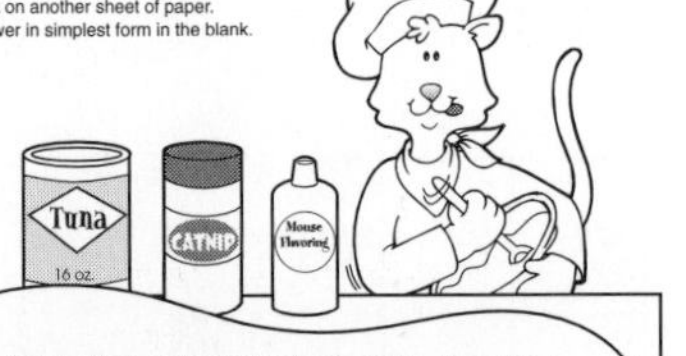

Tuna
16 oz.
CATNIP
Mouse Flavoring

1. Carrie is mixing batter to make fish-shaped pancakes. Her measuring cup has $3\frac{2}{3}$ cups of milk in it. If she pours $2\frac{1}{3}$ cups into the batter, how much milk will be left in the measuring cup? $1\frac{1}{3}$ cups

2. Carlos is making catnip cookies. The recipe calls for $2\frac{3}{8}$ teaspoons of catnip. He has already added $1\frac{1}{8}$ teaspoons. How many more teaspoons of catnip does he need to add? $1\frac{1}{4}$ teaspoons

3. Candie is making mouse-flavored meatloaf. It must cook for $2\frac{3}{4}$ hours. If it has already cooked for $1\frac{1}{4}$ hours, how much longer should it cook? $1\frac{1}{2}$ hours

4. Connor is making tuna casserole. The recipe calls for $7\frac{9}{10}$ ounces of tuna and $3\frac{1}{10}$ ounces of cheese. How many more ounces of tuna than cheese does Connor need? $4\frac{4}{5}$ ounces

5. Cara is decorating a mouse-shaped birthday cake. She needs $2\frac{1}{6}$ cups of sugar for the icing. She added $3\frac{5}{6}$ cups by mistake. How much extra sugar did Cara add? $1\frac{2}{3}$ cups

6. Cal is making a shopping list for next week's cooking class. He needs to buy $10\frac{3}{5}$ pounds of flour and $4\frac{1}{5}$ pounds of sugar. How many more pounds of flour than sugar does Cal need to buy? $6\frac{2}{5}$ pounds

46 Story problems: subtracting mixed numbers with like denominators

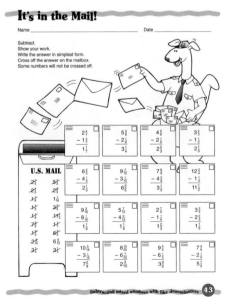

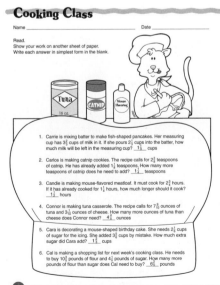

Road Hunting

Name _____ Date _____

Subtract.
Show your work on another sheet of paper.
Write each answer in simplest form.

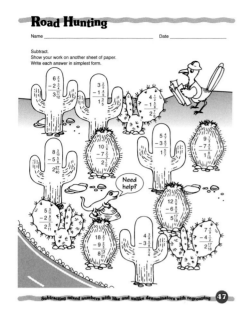

Need help?

Subtracting mixed numbers with like and unlike denominators with regrouping **47**

Treetop Construction

Name _____ Date _____

Read.
Solve each problem on another sheet of paper.
Write each answer in simplest form in the blank provided.

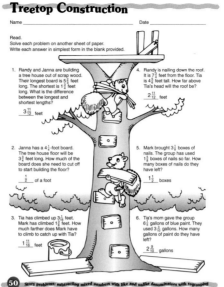

1. Randy and Janna are building a tree house out of scrap wood. Their longest board is $5\frac{5}{6}$ feet long. The shortest is $1\frac{3}{4}$ feet long. What is the difference between the longest and shortest lengths?

$3\frac{11}{12}$ feet

2. Janna has a $4\frac{1}{4}$-foot board. The tree house floor will be $3\frac{3}{4}$ feet long. How much of the board does she need to cut off to start building the floor?

$\frac{1}{2}$ of a foot

3. Tia has climbed up $3\frac{1}{16}$ feet. Mark has climbed $1\frac{7}{8}$ feet. How much farther does Mark have to climb to catch up with Tia?

$1\frac{11}{16}$ feet

4. Randy is nailing down the roof. It is $7\frac{2}{3}$ feet from the floor. Tia is $4\frac{3}{4}$ feet tall. How far above Tia's head will the roof be?

$2\frac{11}{12}$ feet

5. Mark brought $3\frac{1}{6}$ boxes of nails. The group has used $1\frac{5}{8}$ boxes of nails so far. How many boxes of nails do they have left?

$1\frac{1}{2}$ boxes

6. Tia's mom gave the group $6\frac{1}{2}$ gallons of blue paint. They used $3\frac{3}{5}$ gallons. How many gallons of paint do they have left?

$2\frac{9}{10}$ gallons

50 Story problems: subtracting mixed numbers with like and unlike denominators with regrouping

---

Billionaire Baker

Name _____ Date _____

Subtract.
Show your work.
Write the answer in simplest form.
To solve the riddle, match the letters to the numbered lines below.

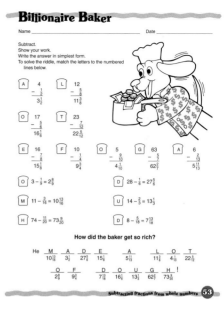

A 4
  $-\frac{2}{3}$
  $3\frac{1}{3}$

L 12
  $-\frac{5}{8}$
  $11\frac{3}{8}$

O 17
  $-\frac{5}{16}$
  $16\frac{5}{16}$

T 23
  $-\frac{1}{22}$
  $22\frac{5}{22}$

E 16
  $-\frac{1}{15}$
  $15\frac{1}{15}$

F 10
  $-\frac{3}{4}$
  $9\frac{3}{4}$

O 5
  $-\frac{9}{10}$
  $4\frac{1}{10}$

G 63
  $-\frac{5}{62}$
  $62\frac{5}{62}$

A 6
  $-\frac{2}{13}$
  $5\frac{11}{13}$

O $3 - \frac{1}{9} = 2\frac{8}{9}$

D $28 - \frac{1}{6} = 27\frac{5}{6}$

M $11 - \frac{3}{16} = 10\frac{13}{16}$

U $14 - \frac{2}{3} = 13\frac{1}{3}$

H $74 - \frac{11}{20} = 73\frac{9}{20}$

D $8 - \frac{5}{13} = 7\frac{13}{13}$

How did the baker get so rich?

He $\underset{10\frac{13}{16}}{M}$ $\underset{3\frac{1}{3}}{A}$ $\underset{27\frac{5}{6}}{D}$ $\underset{15\frac{1}{15}}{E}$ $\underset{5\frac{1}{13}}{A}$ $\underset{11\frac{3}{8}}{L}$ $\underset{4\frac{1}{10}}{O}$ $\underset{22\frac{5}{22}}{T}$

$\underset{2\frac{8}{9}}{O}$ $\underset{9\frac{3}{4}}{F}$ $\underset{7\frac{13}{13}}{D}$ $\underset{16\frac{5}{16}}{O}$ $\underset{2\frac{8}{9}}{U}$ $\underset{73\frac{9}{20}}{G}$ $\underset{}{H}$!

Subtracting fractions from whole numbers **53**

Around We Go!

Name _____ Date _____

Subtract.
Show your work on another sheet of paper.
Write each answer in simplest form.
Color the matching answers.
One number will not be colored.

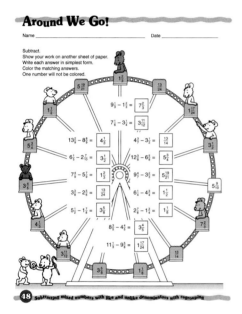

$9\frac{1}{3} - 1\frac{3}{5} = 7\frac{11}{15}$

$7\frac{1}{6} - 3\frac{1}{4} = 3\frac{11}{12}$

$13\frac{1}{6} - 8\frac{5}{6} = 4\frac{1}{3}$

$4\frac{1}{7} - 3\frac{1}{2} = 13\frac{1}{14}$

$6\frac{1}{3} - 2\frac{7}{8} = 3\frac{1}{2}$

$12\frac{3}{8} - 6\frac{8}{9} = 5\frac{3}{4}$

$7\frac{3}{4} - 5\frac{5}{7} = 1\frac{5}{21}$

$9\frac{4}{5} - 3\frac{4}{6} = 5\frac{9}{10}$

$9\frac{3}{8} - 2\frac{4}{5} = 13\frac{2}{14}$

$6\frac{1}{4} - 4\frac{3}{4} = 3\frac{7}{8}$

$5\frac{1}{2} - 1\frac{5}{6} = 3\frac{5}{8}$

$2\frac{1}{8} - 1\frac{1}{4} = 1\frac{7}{8}$

$8\frac{3}{5} - 4\frac{5}{6} = 3\frac{4}{5}$

$11\frac{1}{3} - 9\frac{5}{8} = 1\frac{17}{24}$

48 Subtracting mixed numbers with like and unlike denominators with regrouping

---

Crack a Book!

Name _____ Date _____

Subtract.
Show your work.
Write the answer in simplest form.

This book is great!

15
$-\frac{1}{14}$
$14\frac{1}{14}$

8
$-\frac{2}{9}$
$7\frac{7}{9}$

2
$-\frac{5}{6}$
$1\frac{1}{6}$

36
$-\frac{1}{35}$
$35\frac{1}{35}$

I know. I loved it!

75
$-\frac{1}{4}$
$74\frac{3}{4}$

26
$-\frac{1}{25}$
$25\frac{1}{25}$

52
$-\frac{9}{18}$
$51\frac{1}{2}$

12
$-\frac{1}{11}$
$11\frac{5}{11}$

Who's the author?

1
$-\frac{6}{17}$
$\frac{11}{17}$

46
$-\frac{13}{13}$
$45\frac{5}{13}$

39
$-\frac{5}{8}$
$38\frac{3}{8}$

10
$-\frac{9}{11}$
$9\frac{4}{11}$

62
$-\frac{1}{8}$
$61\frac{1}{8}$

Subtracting fractions from whole numbers **51**

Polly's Pets

Name _____ Date _____

Read.
Solve each problem on another sheet of paper.
Write the answer in simplest form in the blank.

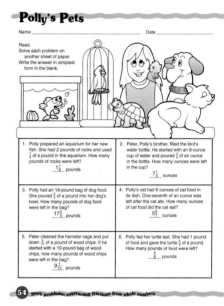

1. Polly prepared an aquarium for her new fish. She had 2 pounds of rocks and used $\frac{1}{8}$ of a pound in the aquarium. How many pounds of rocks were left?

_____ pounds

2. Peter, Polly's brother, filled the bird's water bottle. He started with an 8-ounce cup of water and poured $\frac{3}{4}$ of an ounce in the bottle. How many ounces were left in the cup?

$7\frac{1}{4}$ ounces

3. Polly had an 18-pound bag of dog food. She poured $\frac{2}{3}$ of a pound into her dog's bowl. How many pounds of dog food were left in the bag?

$17\frac{1}{3}$ pounds

4. Polly's cat had 6 ounces of cat food in its dish. One-seventh of an ounce was left after the cat ate. How many ounces of cat food did the cat eat?

$5\frac{6}{7}$ ounces

5. Peter cleaned the hamster cage and put down $\frac{1}{10}$ of a pound of wood chips. If he started with a 10-pound bag of wood chips, how many pounds of wood chips were left in the bag?

$9\frac{9}{10}$ pounds

6. Polly fed her turtle last. She had 1 pound of food and gave the turtle $\frac{1}{9}$ of a pound. How many pounds of food were left?

$\frac{8}{9}$ pounds

54 Story problems: subtracting fractions from whole numbers

If Wishes Were Fishes...

Name _____ Date _____

Subtract.
Show your work on another sheet of paper.
Write each answer in simplest form.
Color by the code.

Color Code
less than 1 = brown
between 1 and 4 = gray
greater than 4 = blue

49 Subtracting mixed numbers with like and unlike denominators with regrouping

---

On Your Mark, Get Set, Go!

Name _____ Date _____

Subtract.
Show your work.
Write the answer in simplest form.
Color the boxes with answers greater than 20 to show the path to the trophy.

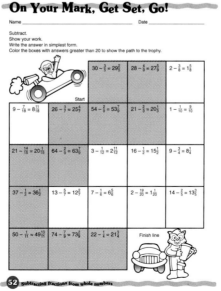

$30 - \frac{1}{6} = 29\frac{5}{6}$

$28 - \frac{1}{5} = 27\frac{4}{5}$

$2 - \frac{1}{6} = 1\frac{5}{6}$

Start

$9 - \frac{7}{18} = 8\frac{11}{18}$

$26 - \frac{2}{7} = 25\frac{5}{7}$

$54 - \frac{2}{9} = 53\frac{7}{9}$

$21 - \frac{2}{3} = 20\frac{1}{3}$

$1 - \frac{1}{10} = \frac{9}{10}$

$21 - \frac{14}{15} = 20\frac{1}{15}$

$64 - \frac{2}{8} = 63\frac{6}{8}$

$3 - \frac{1}{12} = 2\frac{11}{12}$

$16 - \frac{1}{2} = 15\frac{1}{2}$

$9 - \frac{3}{4} = 8\frac{1}{4}$

$37 - \frac{1}{2} = 36\frac{1}{2}$

$13 - \frac{6}{7} = 12\frac{1}{7}$

$7 - \frac{1}{6} = 6\frac{5}{6}$

$2 - \frac{1}{20} = 1\frac{19}{20}$

$14 - \frac{2}{3} = 13\frac{1}{3}$

$50 - \frac{1}{11} = 49\frac{10}{11}$

$74 - \frac{2}{9} = 73\frac{7}{9}$

$22 - \frac{3}{4} = 21\frac{1}{4}$

Finish line

52 Subtracting fractions from whole numbers

Takin' a Break

Name _____ Date _____

Subtract.
Show your work.
Write each answer in simplest form.
Color the matching answer on the wheel.
Some wheels will not be colored.

Barkersville
Rest Stop

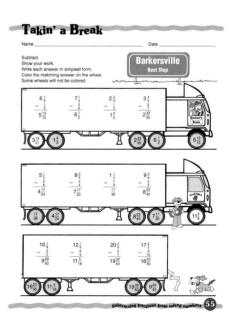

Subtracting fractions from mixed numbers **55**

131

Just Beachy!

Name _____ Date _____

Subtract.
Show your work on another sheet of paper.
Write each answer in simplest form.
Color by the code.

Color Code
less than 2 = yellow
between 2 and 5 = red
greater than 5 = blue

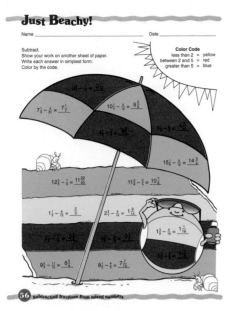

"Haaave" You Heard?

Name _____ Date _____

Multiply.
Show your work.
Write each answer in simplest form.
To solve the riddle, match the letters to the numbered lines below.
Some letters will be used.

Why did the farmer's wife think no one listened to her?

O N L Y   T H E   S H E E P
7/48 2/27 1/18 1/12   7/15 1/15   7/14 7/15 3/8 15/56

" H E R D "   H E R .
7/15 3/8 1/10 3/4

Saturday With Spike

Name _____ Date _____

Read.
Solve each problem on another sheet of paper.
Write each answer in simplest form in the blank.

1. Spike spends all day Saturday working for his dog-walking service. Spike spends 2/3 day walking dogs. He spends 1/2 of that time walking large dogs. What part of a day does Spike spend walking large dogs?
___ day

2. Spike's friend Fifi spends 1/2 day working for Spike. She spends 3/4 of that time walking poodles. What part of a day does Fifi spend walking poodles?
3/8 day

3. Spike uses 1/2 gallon of water for dogs to drink. He gives 1/4 of that water to the small dogs. What part of the gallon does he give to the small dogs?
1/8 gallon

4. Of all the dogs that Spike is walking, 1/2 are not first-time walkers. Of that number, 1/2 of the dogs have walked with Spike two or more times. What part of the group of dogs that Spike is walking have walked with him two or more times?
1/4 group

5. Fifi is collecting information on the group of dogs that Spike walks. She recorded that 2/3 of the dogs are male and 3/5 of those male dogs are puppies. What part of the group of dogs that Spike walks are male puppies?
7/15 group

6. Fifi also noted that 5/6 of the poodles that she walks are white. Of those white poodles, 1/2 are female. What part of the group of poodles that Fifi walks are white females?
5/12 group

Craggy-Croc Skin Solution

Name _____ Date _____

Subtract.
Show your work on another sheet of paper.
Color if correct.
Connect the colored boxes to show the path to the jar.

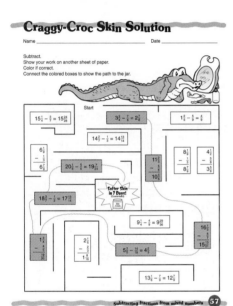

A "Purr-fect" Princess

Name _____ Date _____

Multiply.
Write each answer in simplest form.
Cross off the answer on the towers.
Some answers will not be crossed off.

It's Not Easy!

Name _____ Date _____

Multiply.
Show your work.
Write each answer in simplest form.
Color the matching answer on the giraffe.
Some answers will not be colored.

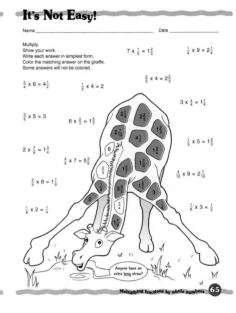

Water Strider on Skis!

Name _____ Date _____

Read.
Solve each problem on another sheet of paper.
Write each answer in simplest form in the blank provided.

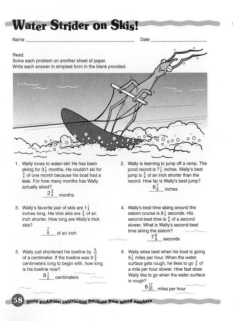

1. Wally loves to water-ski! He has been skiing for 3 1/2 months. He couldn't ski for 3/4 of one month because his boat had a leak. For how many months has Wally actually skied?
2 3/4 months

2. Wally is learning to jump off a ramp. The pond record is 7 1/2 inches. Wally's best jump is 5/8 of an inch shorter than the record. How far is Wally's best jump?
6 7/8 inches

3. Wally's favorite pair of skis are 1 1/4 inches long. His trick skis are 3/8 of an inch shorter. How long are Wally's trick skis?
7/8 of an inch

4. Wally's best time skiing around the slalom course is 8 1/2 seconds. His second-best time is 5/9 of a second slower. What is Wally's second-best time skiing the slalom?
7 7/9 seconds

5. Wally just shortened his towline by 2/10 of a centimeter. If the towline was 9 4/5 centimeters long to begin with, how long is his towline now?
8 1/2 centimeters

6. Wally skies best when his boat is going 9 1/4 miles per hour. When the water surface gets rough, he likes to go 2/3 of a mile per hour slower. How fast does Wally like to go when the water surface is rough?
8 1/12 miles per hour

Love Bugs

Name _____ Date _____

Multiply.
Show your work on another sheet of paper.
Write each answer in simplest form.
Color if correct.

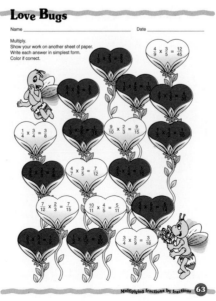

No More Milk

Name _____ Date _____

Multiply.
Show your work.
Write each answer in simplest form.

A 1/3 x 9 = 3
N 10 x 1/4 = 2 1/2
S 1/4 x 7 = 1 3/4

H 2/5 x 7 = 2 4/5
D 5 x 3/8 = 1 7/8
E 3/8 x 2 = 1 1/2

I 5/6 x 6 = 5
R 3 x 1/9 = 1/3
U 2/7 x 14 = 4

A 4 x 7/8 = 3 1/2
E 8 x 3/7 = 3 3/7
R 1/2 x 12 = 2 2/5

L 4/6 x 6 = 4 4/5
S 3 x 1/12 = 1/4
W 4/7 x 4 = 1 7/9
U 5 x 1/10 = 1/2

D 15 x 2/3 = 10
E 7/8 x 8 = 6
A 1/8 x 3 = 3/8
F 9 x 4/7 = 5 1/7

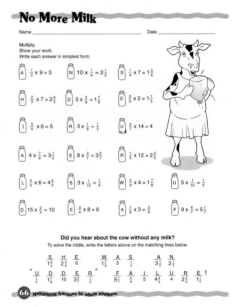

Did you hear about the cow without any milk?
To solve the riddle, write the letters above on the matching lines below.

S H E   W A S   A N
1 1/2 2 4/5 1 1/4   1 3/4 3 1/2 1/4   3 1/2 2 1/2

" U D D E R "   F A I L U R E !
4 2 1 7/8 3 3/7 1/3   5 1/7 3/8 5 4 1/2 1/3 2 2/5

Let's Salsa!

Name _____ Date _____

Multiply.
Show your work on another sheet of paper.
Write each answer in simplest form.
Color the pepper red if correct and green if incorrect.

$\frac{3}{4} \times 6 = 4\frac{1}{2}$ $9 \times \frac{4}{9} = 4\frac{1}{5}$

$\frac{1}{3} \times 12 = 4$ $\frac{3}{5} \times \frac{5}{8} = 8$

$7 \times \frac{4}{5} = 4\frac{3}{5}$ $\frac{1}{4} \times 9 = 3\frac{5}{8}$

$\frac{5}{7} \times \frac{5}{12} = \frac{5}{84}$ $\frac{3}{10} \times 4 = \frac{2}{5}$ $\frac{1}{6} \times 4 = \frac{2}{3}$

$3 \times \frac{5}{6} = 1\frac{5}{6}$ $\frac{1}{3} \times \frac{5}{7} = \frac{5}{21}$ $\frac{1}{5} \times 11 = 1\frac{1}{7}$

$\frac{5}{12} \times 10 = 7$ $15 \times \frac{1}{3} = 5$ $\frac{5}{7} \times \frac{2}{3} = \frac{2}{21}$

$\frac{1}{3} \times 3 = \frac{1}{27}$ $3 \times \frac{3}{5}$

$\frac{4}{9} \times 7 = 3\frac{5}{9}$ $\frac{3}{5} \times 2 = 1\frac{1}{5}$

Sail Away!

Name _____ Date _____

Multiply.
Show your work.
Write each answer in simplest form.
Color by the code.

Color Code
less than 1 = blue
between 1 and 5 = yellow
greater than 5 = brown

$\frac{1}{2} \times 12\frac{1}{2} = 6\frac{1}{4}$

$\frac{5}{9} \times 2\frac{1}{4} = 1\frac{7}{8}$

$\frac{2}{3} \times 4\frac{4}{9} = 3\frac{1}{3}$ $\frac{7}{8} \times 2\frac{1}{5} = \frac{7}{16}$

$\frac{3}{5} \times 1\frac{1}{10} = \frac{13}{80}$ $\frac{4}{7} \times 5\frac{3}{4} = 3\frac{13}{21}$

$\frac{1}{6} \times 15\frac{3}{8} = 6\frac{7}{8}$ $\frac{1}{4} \times 3\frac{1}{9} = \frac{13}{14}$

$\frac{6}{7} \times 10\frac{1}{2} = 9$ $\frac{7}{8} \times 14\frac{1}{3} = 6\frac{1}{16}$ $\frac{2}{5} \times 7\frac{1}{6} = 2\frac{5}{9}$

$\frac{5}{8} \times 8\frac{2}{3} = 5\frac{5}{12}$ $\frac{4}{9} \times 11\frac{2}{3} = 5\frac{1}{18}$

$\frac{3}{10} \times 1\frac{1}{6} = \frac{7}{20}$

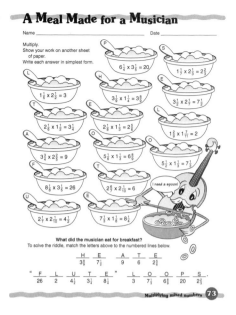

A Meal Made for a Musician

Name _____ Date _____

Multiply.
Show your work on another sheet of paper.
Write each answer in simplest form.

P $6\frac{1}{4} \times 3\frac{1}{5} = 20$ S

L $1\frac{1}{3} \times 2\frac{1}{2} = 2\frac{5}{8}$

$1\frac{1}{8} \times 2\frac{1}{4} = 3$ H $3\frac{5}{8} \times 1\frac{1}{4} = 3\frac{5}{8}$ E $3\frac{1}{2} \times 2\frac{1}{7} = 7\frac{1}{2}$

$2\frac{5}{8} \times 1\frac{1}{3} = 3\frac{1}{2}$ A $2\frac{1}{4} \times 1\frac{1}{2} = 3\frac{3}{8}$ $3\frac{1}{2} \times 1\frac{7}{11} = 2\frac{5}{8}$ L

$3\frac{3}{4} \times 2\frac{2}{5} = 9$ $5\frac{1}{4} \times 1\frac{1}{3} = 7\frac{1}{3}$ O

$8\frac{1}{8} \times 3\frac{1}{5} = 26$ F   T $2\frac{6}{9} \times 2\frac{1}{10} = 6$

U $2\frac{1}{7} \times 2\frac{1}{10} = 4\frac{1}{2}$ E $7\frac{1}{8} \times 1\frac{1}{8} = 8\frac{1}{4}$

What did the musician eat for breakfast?
To solve the riddle, match the letters above to the numbered lines below.

H   E   A   T   E
$\overline{3\frac{5}{8}}$ $\overline{7\frac{1}{3}}$ $\overline{9}$ $\overline{6}$ $\overline{3\frac{1}{2}}$

" F   L   U   T   E "   L   O   O   P   S
$\overline{26}$ $\overline{4\frac{1}{2}}$ $\overline{3\frac{3}{8}}$ $\overline{8\frac{1}{4}}$ $\overline{3}$ $\overline{60}$ $\overline{20}$ $\overline{2\frac{5}{8}}$

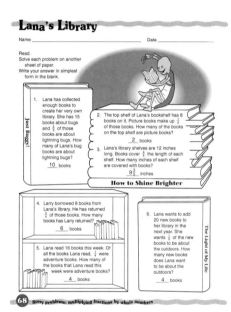

Lana's Library

Name _____ Date _____

Read.
Solve each problem on another sheet of paper.
Write your answer in simplest form in the blank.

Just Buggy!

1. Lana has collected enough books to create her very own library. She has 15 books about bugs and $\frac{2}{3}$ of those books are about lightning bugs. How many of Lana's bug books are about lightning bugs?
   10 books

2. The top shelf of Lana's bookshelf has 8 books on it. Picture books make up $\frac{1}{4}$ of those books. How many of the books on the top shelf are picture books?
   2 books

3. Lana's library shelves are 12 inches long. Books cover $\frac{5}{6}$ the length of each shelf. How many inches of each shelf are covered with books?
   9$\frac{3}{5}$ inches

How to Shine Brighter

4. Larry borrowed 8 books from Lana's library. He has returned $\frac{3}{4}$ of those books. How many books has Larry returned?
   6 books

5. Lana read 16 books this week. Of all the books Lana read, $\frac{1}{4}$ were adventure books. How many of the books that Lana read this week were adventure books?
   4 books

6. Lana wants to add 20 new books to her library in the next year. She wants $\frac{1}{5}$ of the new books to be about the outdoors. How many new books does Lana want to be about the outdoors?
   4 books

The Light of My Life

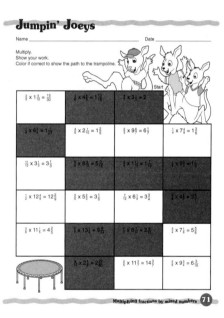

Jumpin' Joeys

Name _____ Date _____

Multiply.
Show your work.
Color if correct to show the path to the trampoline.

Start

$\frac{5}{6} \times 1\frac{1}{10} = \frac{15}{30}$ $\frac{5}{8} \times 4\frac{1}{4} = 1\frac{3}{16}$ $\frac{1}{4} \times 3\frac{1}{2} = 2$

$\frac{4}{7} \times 6\frac{1}{2} = 1\frac{1}{27}$ $\frac{2}{5} \times 2\frac{1}{10} = 1\frac{2}{5}$ $\frac{4}{9} \times 9\frac{5}{6} = 6\frac{1}{7}$ $\frac{1}{4} \times 7\frac{1}{6} = 1\frac{5}{6}$

$\frac{11}{12} \times 3\frac{1}{4} = 3\frac{1}{3}$ $\frac{3}{5} \times 8\frac{2}{3} = 5\frac{1}{12}$ $\frac{4}{5} \times 1\frac{1}{3} = 1\frac{7}{9}$ $\frac{3}{4} \times 8\frac{1}{3} = 1\frac{1}{12}$

$\frac{1}{8} \times 12\frac{1}{3} = 12\frac{2}{9}$ $\frac{2}{5} \times 5\frac{1}{3} = 3\frac{1}{6}$ $\frac{7}{12} \times 6\frac{1}{4} = 3\frac{3}{4}$ $\frac{3}{4} \times 4\frac{1}{4} = 3\frac{3}{4}$

$\frac{1}{3} \times 11\frac{1}{4} = 4\frac{5}{6}$ $\frac{1}{4} \times 13\frac{1}{3} = 9\frac{2}{4}$ $\frac{1}{5} \times 8\frac{1}{4} = 2\frac{2}{6}$ $\frac{1}{3} \times 7\frac{1}{2} = 5\frac{2}{3}$

$\frac{7}{8} \times 2\frac{1}{3} = 2\frac{8}{800}$ $\frac{3}{4} \times 11\frac{2}{3} = 14\frac{3}{4}$ $\frac{2}{3} \times 9\frac{1}{4} = 6\frac{3}{16}$

Cheer Gear

Name _____ Date _____

Multiply.
Show your work.
Write each answer in simplest form.

$2\frac{1}{3} \times 1\frac{1}{2} = 2\frac{6}{7}$

$1\frac{1}{3} \times 3\frac{1}{4} = 3\frac{7}{8}$

$2\frac{1}{4} \times 3\frac{1}{3} = 7\frac{1}{2}$ $3\frac{1}{3} \times 3\frac{1}{4} = 11$ $2\frac{1}{5} \times 2\frac{1}{2} = 6\frac{2}{5}$

$4\frac{1}{3} \times 4\frac{1}{8} = 17\frac{1}{2}$ $6\frac{1}{4} \times 1\frac{1}{6} = 7\frac{1}{2}$

$1\frac{1}{3} \times 1\frac{5}{6} = 2\frac{4}{9}$ $5\frac{5}{8} \times 2\frac{1}{4} = 12\frac{5}{8}$

$2\frac{2}{3} \times 3\frac{1}{8} = 8\frac{1}{3}$ $6\frac{1}{4} \times 1\frac{1}{2} = 9\frac{3}{4}$

$1\frac{1}{3} \times 5\frac{1}{2} = 5\frac{3}{6}$ $4\frac{2}{3} \times 2\frac{1}{7} = 10$ $1\frac{1}{9} \times 1\frac{1}{4} = 1\frac{3}{8}$

$1\frac{1}{3} \times 3\frac{1}{2} = 4\frac{1}{3}$ $1\frac{1}{11} \times 1\frac{1}{4} = 1\frac{3}{11}$

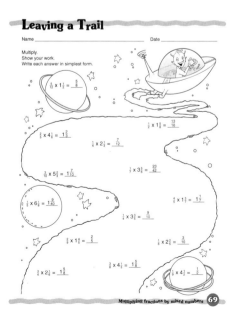

Leaving a Trail

Name _____ Date _____

Multiply.
Show your work.
Write each answer in simplest form.

$\frac{5}{12} \times 1\frac{1}{2} = $

$\frac{2}{5} \times 4\frac{1}{8} = 1\frac{3}{5}$

$\frac{1}{4} \times 2\frac{1}{3} = \frac{7}{12}$

$\frac{2}{9} \times 5\frac{1}{4} = 1\frac{1}{10}$ $\frac{1}{7} \times 3\frac{1}{6} = \frac{23}{42}$

$\frac{1}{5} \times 6\frac{1}{8} = 1\frac{9}{40}$ $\frac{4}{9} \times 1\frac{1}{3} = 1\frac{1}{2}$

$\frac{1}{5} \times 4\frac{1}{8} = \frac{2}{5}$ $\frac{1}{4} \times 3\frac{1}{5} = \frac{9}{10}$ $\frac{1}{4} \times 1\frac{1}{5} = \frac{3}{10}$

$\frac{5}{9} \times 1\frac{1}{4} = \frac{5}{6}$ $\frac{3}{4} \times 4\frac{1}{3} = 1\frac{5}{6}$

$\frac{1}{3} \times 2\frac{1}{8} = 1\frac{1}{9}$ $\frac{8}{9} \times 4\frac{1}{5} = 1\frac{5}{8}$

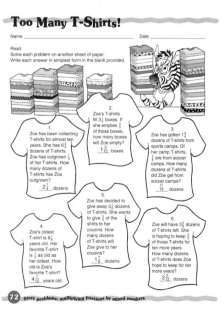

Too Many T-Shirts!

Name _____ Date _____

Read.
Solve each problem on another sheet of paper.
Write each answer in simplest form in the blank provided.

1. Zoe has been collecting T-shirts for almost ten years. She has $6\frac{3}{4}$ dozens of T-shirts. Zoe has outgrown $\frac{1}{3}$ of her T-shirts. How many dozens of T-shirts has Zoe outgrown?
   2$\frac{1}{4}$ dozens

2. Zoe's T-shirts fill $3\frac{1}{4}$ boxes. If she empties $\frac{2}{5}$ of those boxes, how many boxes will Zoe empty?
   1$\frac{3}{10}$ boxes

3. Zoe has gotten $1\frac{5}{6}$ dozens of T-shirts from sports camps. Of her camp T-shirts, $\frac{3}{10}$ are from soccer camps. How many dozens of T-shirts did Zoe get from soccer camps?
   $\frac{11}{16}$ dozens

4. Zoe's oldest T-shirt is $9\frac{1}{2}$ years old. Her favorite T-shirt is $\frac{1}{2}$ as old as her oldest. How old is Zoe's favorite T-shirt?
   4$\frac{12}{12}$ years old

5. Zoe has decided to give away $3\frac{1}{2}$ dozens of T-shirts. She wants to give $\frac{1}{3}$ of the shirts to her cousins. How many dozens of T-shirts will Zoe give to her cousins?
   1$\frac{1}{8}$ dozens

6. Zoe will have $3\frac{2}{3}$ dozens of T-shirts left. She is hoping to keep $\frac{5}{8}$ of those T-shirts for ten more years. How many dozens of T-shirts does Zoe hope to keep for ten more years?
   2$\frac{5}{12}$ dozens

All You Can Eat

Name _____ Date _____

Multiply.
Show your work.
Write each answer in simplest form.
Color the boxes with answers less than 20 to show the path to the buffet.

Start

$3\frac{1}{3} \times 2\frac{1}{8} = 6\frac{3}{16}$ $2\frac{7}{12} \times 4\frac{8}{9} = 12\frac{5}{8}$ $9\frac{4}{5} \times 2\frac{1}{10} = 18\frac{17}{10}$

$9\frac{1}{6} \times 4\frac{1}{2} = 41\frac{1}{4}$ $11\frac{1}{8} \times 2\frac{1}{4} = 26\frac{1}{8}$ $6\frac{1}{3} \times 3\frac{5}{6} = 23\frac{5}{8}$ $4\frac{3}{4} \times 4\frac{1}{12} = 17\frac{1}{2}$

$17\frac{1}{3} \times 3\frac{3}{8} = 63$ $21\frac{1}{4} \times 1\frac{1}{12} = 34\frac{21}{24}$ $1\frac{1}{2} \times 11\frac{3}{8} = 17\frac{5}{10}$ $3\frac{1}{10} \times 2\frac{3}{8} = 7\frac{7}{20}$

$8\frac{1}{4} \times 3\frac{1}{2} = 28\frac{7}{8}$ $8\frac{1}{4} \times 6\frac{1}{2} = 55$ $5\frac{1}{3} \times 3\frac{1}{2} = 16$

BAMBOO BUFFET

Track and Field Feats

Name _____ Date _____

Read.
Show your work on another sheet of paper.
Write each answer in simplest form in the blank.

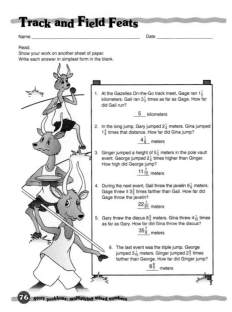

1. At the Gazelles On-the-Go track meet, Gage ran $1\frac{1}{4}$ kilometers. Gail ran $3\frac{1}{3}$ times as far as Gage. How far did Gail run?

   _5_ kilometers

2. In the long jump, Gary jumped $2\frac{1}{4}$ meters. Gina jumped $1\frac{5}{6}$ times that distance. How far did Gina jump?

   $4\frac{1}{8}$ meters

3. Ginger jumped a height of $5\frac{1}{2}$ meters in the pole vault event. George jumped $2\frac{1}{5}$ times higher than Ginger. How high did George jump?

   $11\frac{7}{10}$ meters

4. During the next event, Gail threw the javelin $6\frac{1}{4}$ meters. Gage threw it $3\frac{3}{5}$ times farther than Gail. How far did Gage throw the javelin?

   $22\frac{1}{20}$ meters

5. Gary threw the discus $8\frac{1}{4}$ meters. Gina threw $4\frac{1}{10}$ times as far as Gary. How far did Gina throw the discus?

   $35\frac{7}{8}$ meters

6. The last event was the triple jump. George jumped $3\frac{1}{10}$ meters. Ginger jumped $2\frac{5}{6}$ times farther than George. How far did Ginger jump?

   $8\frac{6}{7}$ meters

Where's My Bone?

Name _____ Date _____

Divide.
Show your work on another sheet of paper.
Color if correct.
Connect the colored boxes to show the path to the bone.

I know I buried it here somewhere!

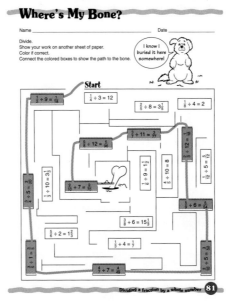

Start

$\frac{1}{2} \div 9 = \frac{1}{18}$

$\frac{1}{4} \div 3 = 12$

$\frac{2}{5} \div 8 = 3\frac{1}{5}$

$\frac{1}{5} \div 4 = 2$

$\frac{3}{4} \div 11 = \frac{3}{44}$

$\frac{5}{6} \div 12 = \frac{1}{5}$

$\frac{7}{8} \div 12 = \frac{1}{16}$

$\frac{2}{3} \div 5 = 3\frac{1}{3}$

$\frac{2}{3} \div 7 = \frac{2}{21}$

$\frac{3}{4} \div 6 = 15\frac{1}{3}$

$\frac{5}{6} \div 2 = 1\frac{2}{3}$

$\frac{1}{3} \div 4 = \frac{1}{7}$

$\frac{4}{7} \div 7 = \frac{4}{49}$

Birthday Bash Crash

Name _____ Date _____

Read.
Show your work on another sheet of paper.
Write each answer in simplest form in the blank provided.

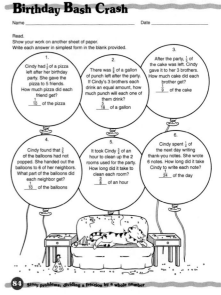

1. Cindy had $\frac{1}{2}$ of a pizza left after her birthday party. She gave the pizza to 5 friends. How much pizza did each friend get?

   $\frac{1}{10}$ of the pizza

2. There was $\frac{3}{5}$ of a gallon of punch left after the party. If Cindy's 3 brothers each drink an equal amount, how much punch will each one of them drink?

   $\frac{1}{5}$ of a gallon

3. After the party, $\frac{1}{3}$ of the cake was left. Cindy gave it to her 3 brothers. How much cake did each brother get?

   $\frac{1}{9}$ of the cake

4. Cindy found that $\frac{2}{5}$ of the balloons had not popped. She handed out the balloons to 6 of her neighbors. What part of the balloons did each neighbor get?

   $\frac{1}{10}$ of the balloons

5. It took Cindy $\frac{2}{3}$ of an hour to clean up the 2 rooms used for the party. How long did it take to clean each room?

   $\frac{1}{3}$ of an hour

6. Cindy spent $\frac{1}{4}$ of the next day writing thank-you notes. She wrote 6 notes. How long did it take Cindy to write each note?

   $\frac{1}{24}$ of the day

Team Spirit

Name _____ Date _____

Divide.
Show your work.
Write each answer in simplest form.

Give me a D!

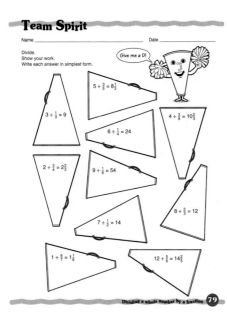

$3 \div \frac{1}{3} = 9$

$5 \div \frac{3}{5} = 8\frac{1}{3}$

$4 \div \frac{3}{8} = 10\frac{2}{3}$

$6 \div \frac{1}{4} = 24$

$2 \div \frac{3}{4} = 2\frac{2}{3}$

$9 \div \frac{1}{6} = 54$

$7 \div \frac{1}{2} = 14$

$8 \div \frac{2}{3} = 12$

$1 \div \frac{6}{7} = 1\frac{1}{6}$

$12 \div \frac{5}{6} = 14\frac{2}{5}$

Bumper Boat Blunder

Name _____ Date _____

Divide.
Show your work on another sheet of paper.
Write each answer in simplest form.

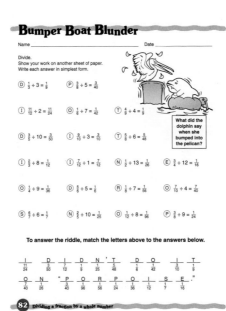

What did the dolphin say when she bumped into the pelican?

(D) $\frac{1}{3} \div 3 = \frac{1}{9}$ (P) $\frac{3}{8} \div 5 = \frac{3}{40}$

(I) $\frac{11}{12} \div 2 = \frac{11}{24}$ (O) $\frac{1}{6} \div 7 = \frac{1}{42}$ (T) $\frac{4}{9} \div 4 = \frac{1}{9}$

(D) $\frac{3}{5} \div 10 = \frac{3}{50}$ (O) $\frac{9}{10} \div 3 = \frac{3}{10}$ (T) $\frac{5}{6} \div 6 = \frac{5}{48}$

(I) $\frac{5}{8} \div 8 = \frac{5}{12}$ (I) $\frac{7}{12} \div 1 = \frac{7}{12}$ (N) $\frac{1}{2} \div 13 = \frac{1}{26}$ (E) $\frac{3}{4} \div 12 = \frac{1}{16}$

(O) $\frac{1}{4} \div 9 = \frac{1}{36}$ (D) $\frac{5}{6} \div 5 = \frac{1}{6}$ (R) $\frac{7}{8} \div 7 = \frac{1}{56}$ (O) $\frac{7}{10} \div 4 = \frac{7}{40}$

(S) $\frac{6}{7} \div 6 = \frac{1}{7}$ (N) $\frac{5}{2} \div 10 = \frac{1}{25}$ (O) $\frac{1}{12} \div 8 = \frac{1}{96}$ (P) $\frac{3}{8} \div 9 = \frac{1}{24}$

To answer the riddle, match the letters above to the answers below.

I D I D N' T D O I T
$\frac{1}{24}$ $\frac{3}{50}$ $\frac{1}{3}$ $\frac{1}{26}$ $\frac{7}{40}$ $\frac{1}{96}$ $\frac{1}{56}$ $\frac{1}{24}$ $\frac{1}{9}$ $\frac{1}{16}$

O N " P O R P O I S E ."
$\frac{7}{40}$ $\frac{1}{26}$ $\frac{3}{40}$ $\frac{1}{96}$ $\frac{1}{56}$ $\frac{1}{24}$ $\frac{1}{36}$ $\frac{7}{12}$ $\frac{1}{7}$ $\frac{1}{16}$

Bird's-Eye View

Name _____ Date _____

Divide.
Show your work.
Write each answer in simplest form.

What a great shot!

$\frac{1}{4} \div \frac{1}{8} = 2$ $\frac{3}{7} \div \frac{1}{5} = 2\frac{1}{7}$ $\frac{3}{8} \div \frac{1}{6} = 4$

$\frac{3}{8} \div \frac{3}{12} = 1\frac{1}{2}$ $\frac{3}{10} \div \frac{3}{9} = 2\frac{7}{10}$ $\frac{1}{4} \div \frac{7}{8} = \frac{2}{7}$ $\frac{4}{5} \div \frac{4}{6} = 1\frac{1}{5}$

$\frac{7}{12} \div \frac{3}{4} = 1\frac{1}{4}$ $\frac{8}{15} \div \frac{2}{5} = 2\frac{2}{5}$ $\frac{4}{11} \div \frac{2}{5} = 1\frac{5}{11}$ $\frac{5}{16} \div \frac{1}{4} = 13\frac{1}{3}$

$\frac{5}{6} \div \frac{2}{3} = 1\frac{1}{4}$ $\frac{3}{4} \div \frac{4}{5} = 2\frac{1}{3}$ $\frac{7}{8} \div \frac{1}{4} = 1\frac{2}{3}$

It's All Downhill From Here!

Name _____ Date _____

Divide.
Show your work.
Write each answer in simplest form.
Cross off the matching answer in the answer bank.
Some answers will not be crossed off.

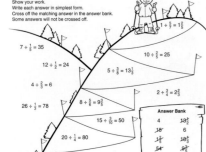

$\frac{1}{4} \div \frac{1}{4} = 1\frac{1}{2}$

$7 \div \frac{1}{5} = 35$

$10 \div \frac{2}{5} = 25$

$12 \div \frac{1}{2} = 24$

$5 \div \frac{3}{8} = 13\frac{1}{3}$

$4 \div \frac{2}{3} = 6$

$2 \div \frac{3}{4} = 2\frac{2}{3}$

$26 \div \frac{1}{3} = 78$

$8 \div \frac{5}{6} = 9\frac{3}{5}$

$15 \div \frac{3}{10} = 50$

$20 \div \frac{1}{4} = 80$

$9 \div \frac{1}{6} = 54$

$13 \div \frac{5}{8} = 20\frac{4}{5}$

$3 \div \frac{2}{9} = 13\frac{1}{2}$

$14 \div \frac{1}{8} = 112$

$12 \div \frac{4}{5} = 15$

$11 \div \frac{3}{5} = 18\frac{1}{3}$

$16 \div \frac{1}{10} = 160$

Answer Bank

4	$18\frac{1}{3}$
18	6
$1\frac{1}{2}$	$18\frac{2}{3}$
54	$9\frac{3}{5}$
8	35
$1\frac{1}{3}$	180
78	$13\frac{1}{2}$
25	80
80	24
	$20\frac{4}{5}$

"A-moose-ment" Park Fun

Name _____ Date _____

Read.
Show your work on another sheet of paper.
Write each answer in simplest form in the blank provided.

1. Matt earned 5 free tickets to Moose Mountain by selling candy bars. If he earned $\frac{1}{3}$ of a ticket for every candy bar he sold, how many candy bars did Matt sell?

   _15_ candy bars

2. Matt and his family plan to spend 6 hours at the park. They decide to meet at the Ice Creamery every $\frac{2}{3}$ of an hour to check in. How many times do Matt and his family plan to meet?

   _9_ times

3. Matt and Maria stood in line for 18 minutes before they got to ride the Cliffs roller coaster. The ride lasted $\frac{3}{4}$ of a minute. How many times could Matt and Maria have ridden the Cliffs during the time they were standing in line?

   _24_ times

4. The Cliffs roller coaster has 2 miles of track. There is either a steep climb, a fast drop, or a sharp turn every $\frac{1}{8}$ of a mile. How many times does the track climb, drop, or turn?

   _16_ times

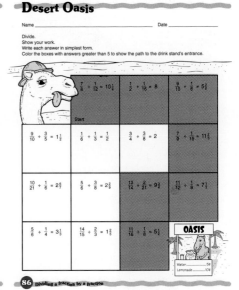

5. Matt bought 3 pounds of peanuts to share with his family. If they ate $\frac{4}{5}$ of a pound every hour, how long would the peanuts last?

   $3\frac{3}{4}$ hours

6. There are 8 miles of paths at Moose Mountain. Drink stands are stationed every $\frac{2}{5}$ of a mile. How many drink stands are there in Moose Mountain?

   _20_ drink stands

The Cliffs

Desert Oasis

Name _____ Date _____

Divide.
Show your work.
Write each answer in simplest form.
Color the boxes with answers greater than 5 to show the path to the drink stand's entrance.

$7\frac{1}{2} \div \frac{1}{2} = 10\frac{1}{2}$ **Start**	$\frac{1}{2} \div \frac{1}{16} = 8$	$\frac{9}{10} \div \frac{1}{8} = 5\frac{2}{9}$
$\frac{9}{10} \div \frac{3}{5} = 1\frac{1}{2}$	$\frac{1}{6} \div \frac{1}{3} = \frac{1}{2}$	$\frac{3}{4} \div \frac{3}{8} = 2$	$\frac{7}{9} \div \frac{1}{15} = 11\frac{2}{3}$
$\frac{10}{21} \div \frac{1}{6} = 2\frac{6}{7}$	$\frac{5}{6} \div \frac{3}{8} = 2\frac{2}{9}$	$\frac{19}{14} \div \frac{2}{21} \approx 9\frac{2}{7}$	$\frac{11}{12} \div \frac{1}{8} = 7\frac{1}{3}$
$\frac{5}{6} \div \frac{1}{4} = 3\frac{1}{3}$	$\frac{14}{15} \div \frac{2}{3} = 1\frac{2}{5}$	$\frac{11}{16} \div \frac{1}{8} = 5\frac{1}{2}$	**OASIS** Water....5¢ Lemonade...10¢

Polar Pops

Name _____ Date _____

Divide.
Show your work.
Write each answer in simplest form.
Cross off the answer on the polar bear.
Some numbers will not be crossed off.

$\frac{3}{4} \div \frac{1}{2} = 1\frac{1}{2}$ $\frac{5}{6} \div \frac{1}{3} = 2\frac{1}{2}$

$\frac{1}{8} \div \frac{3}{4} = \frac{1}{6}$ $\frac{4}{5} \div \frac{1}{10} = 8$

$\frac{6}{7} \div \frac{1}{14} = 12$ $\frac{7}{9} \div \frac{1}{6} = 4\frac{2}{3}$

$\frac{5}{8} \div \frac{10}{17} = 1\frac{1}{16}$ $\frac{3}{5} \div \frac{9}{14} = \frac{14}{15}$

$\frac{7}{8} \div \frac{1}{2} = 1\frac{3}{4}$ $\frac{4}{5} \div \frac{1}{4} = 3\frac{1}{5}$

$\frac{3}{8} \div \frac{9}{10} = \frac{5}{12}$ $\frac{2}{3} \div \frac{7}{15} = 1\frac{3}{7}$

$\frac{19}{20} \div \frac{3}{10} = 3\frac{1}{6}$ $\frac{7}{10} \div \frac{1}{5} = 3\frac{1}{2}$

$\frac{2}{3} \div \frac{2}{15} = 5$ $\frac{9}{14} \div \frac{1}{7} = 4\frac{1}{2}$

$\frac{8}{9} \div \frac{1}{6} = 5\frac{1}{3}$

Surf's Up!

Name _____ Date _____

Divide.
Show your work.
Write each answer in simplest form.

Kowabunga!

Color Code
greater than 4 = blue
between 2 and 4 = yellow
less than 2 = green

$4\frac{1}{2} \div 1\frac{1}{5} = 3\frac{3}{4}$

$6\frac{2}{3} \div 1\frac{1}{3} = 5$

$8\frac{1}{3} \div 1\frac{7}{8} = 4\frac{4}{9}$

$11\frac{2}{3} \div 2\frac{1}{2} = 4\frac{2}{3}$

$3\frac{1}{3} \div 1\frac{2}{6} = 2\frac{6}{7}$

$7\frac{1}{2} \div 1\frac{1}{4} = 6$

$5\frac{1}{4} \div 1\frac{3}{8} = 3\frac{9}{11}$

$4\frac{2}{3} \div 1\frac{3}{4} = 2\frac{2}{3}$

$6\frac{1}{4} \div 1\frac{2}{3} = 3\frac{3}{4}$

$4\frac{2}{3} \div 1\frac{2}{6} = 3\frac{1}{3}$

$3\frac{1}{3} \div 2\frac{5}{6} = 1\frac{2}{6}$

$5\frac{1}{3} \div 3\frac{1}{4} = 1\frac{5}{6}$

$5\frac{1}{4} \div 1\frac{3}{4} = 3$

$10\frac{2}{3} \div 1\frac{9}{6} = 5\frac{9}{11}$

$13\frac{1}{2} \div 2\frac{1}{4} = 6$

Cool Cat Costumes

Name _____ Date _____

Read.
Show your work on another sheet of paper.
Write each answer in simplest form in the blank.

COOL CAT COSTUME SHOP

1. At the Cool Cat Costume Shop, Chris is making lion costumes. He has $\frac{1}{2}$ of a yard of felt. If he needs $\frac{1}{4}$ of a yard of felt for each costume, how many costumes can he make? __2__ costumes

2. Carol is cutting material for milkman costumes. She has $\frac{1}{3}$ of a yard of cotton. If she needs $\frac{1}{9}$ of a yard of cotton for each shirt, how many shirts can she make? __3__ shirts

3. Carl is gluing together orange foam for cheese costumes. He has $\frac{7}{8}$ of a yard of foam and needs $\frac{1}{8}$ of a yard for each costume. How many costumes can he make? __7__ costumes

4. Callie is working on special dogcatcher costumes for some of her friends. She has $\frac{1}{2}$ of a yard of brown material. If she needs $\frac{1}{6}$ of a yard of material for each pair of pants, how many pairs of pants can she make? __3__ pairs

5. Clay is making nets for fisherman costumes. He has $\frac{2}{3}$ of a yard of netting. If he needs $\frac{1}{12}$ of a yard of netting for each net, how many nets can he make? __8__ nets

6. Caroline is measuring material for the fisherman costumes. She has $\frac{5}{6}$ of a yard of fabric for the shirts. If she needs $\frac{1}{12}$ of a yard of fabric for each shirt, how many shirts can she make? __10__ shirts

---

A "Reel-y" Good Movie

Name _____ Date _____

Divide.
Show your work.
Write each answer in simplest form.
Color the popcorn piece with the matching answer.
Some popcorn pieces will not be colored.

They're showing my favorite!   Want some popcorn?

$3\frac{3}{5} \div 1\frac{1}{10} = 3\frac{3}{11}$ $10\frac{1}{2} \div 2\frac{1}{3} = 4\frac{1}{2}$ $6\frac{1}{2} \div 3\frac{1}{2} = 1\frac{6}{7}$

POPCORN

$4\frac{1}{2} \div 2\frac{2}{5} = 1\frac{7}{8}$ $7\frac{1}{7} \div 3\frac{1}{3} = 2\frac{1}{7}$ $3\frac{1}{2} \div 1\frac{3}{11} = 2\frac{3}{4}$

$11\frac{2}{3} \div 1\frac{2}{3} = 7$ $5\frac{3}{5} \div 4\frac{2}{3} = 1\frac{1}{5}$ $8\frac{4}{5} \div 2\frac{4}{9} = 3\frac{3}{5}$

$8\frac{4}{7} \div 6\frac{2}{3} = 1\frac{2}{7}$ $6\frac{4}{7} \div 4\frac{1}{4} = 1\frac{3}{5}$ $7\frac{1}{2} \div 2\frac{4}{5} = 2\frac{4}{5}$

$6\frac{3}{7} \div 4\frac{1}{2} = 1\frac{3}{7}$ $9\frac{1}{3} \div 5\frac{3}{5} = 1\frac{2}{3}$ $6\frac{3}{4} \div 1\frac{1}{8} = 6$

$10\frac{1}{2} \div 4\frac{2}{3} = 2\frac{1}{4}$ $6\frac{3}{4} \div 4\frac{1}{2} = 1\frac{1}{2}$ $7\frac{1}{3} \div 2\frac{3}{4} = 2\frac{2}{3}$

Don't "Bee" Late!

Name _____ Date _____

Divide.
Show your work.
Write each answer in simplest form.

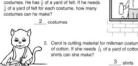

T $4\frac{1}{2} \div 1\frac{1}{2} = 3$ H $3\frac{1}{4} \div 2\frac{3}{5} = 1\frac{1}{4}$ Z $3\frac{1}{7} \div 1\frac{4}{7} = 2$

H $3\frac{1}{4} \div 1\frac{1}{8} = 2\frac{8}{9}$ A $5\frac{1}{2} \div 1\frac{1}{8} = 4\frac{8}{9}$ E $2\frac{1}{4} \div 2\frac{1}{4} = 1\frac{1}{9}$

E $4\frac{1}{8} \div 3\frac{2}{3} = 1\frac{1}{8}$ K $2\frac{2}{5} \div 1\frac{1}{5} = 2\frac{2}{5}$ B $4\frac{1}{2} \div 1\frac{7}{8} = 2\frac{2}{5}$

T $2\frac{1}{10} \div 1\frac{2}{5} = 1\frac{1}{2}$ E $2\frac{1}{3} \div 1\frac{1}{6} = 2\frac{2}{7}$ S $2\frac{2}{3} \div 1\frac{1}{3} = 1\frac{4}{5}$

Z $3\frac{3}{4} \div 1\frac{1}{4} = 3\frac{3}{5}$ U $4\frac{2}{3} \div 1\frac{1}{6} = 4$

BUSY BEE SCHOOL

How does the bee get to school each day?

To solve the riddle, match the letters above to the numbered lines below.

$\underset{2\frac{2}{9}}{H}\ \underset{2\frac{2}{7}}{E}$ $\underset{3}{T}\ \underset{4\frac{8}{9}}{A}\ \underset{1\frac{1}{4}}{K}\ \underset{2\frac{2}{5}}{E}\ \underset{1\frac{1}{2}}{S}$ $\underset{1\frac{1}{9}}{T}\ \underset{1\frac{1}{8}}{H}\ \underset{1\frac{1}{9}}{E}$ $\underset{2\frac{2}{5}}{"B}\ \underset{4}{U}\ \underset{3\frac{3}{5}}{Z}\ \underset{2}{Z}"!$

Digging the Vacation

Name _____ Date _____

Read.
Show your work on another sheet of paper.
Write each answer in simplest form in the blank.

1. The Dalmatian family drove to the beach for a vacation. The family drove $10\frac{1}{2}$ hours to get there. If the family took a break every $3\frac{1}{2}$ hours, how many times did they stop? __3__ times

2. On the first day, Dexter and his sister Dolly were on the beach for $5\frac{1}{4}$ hours. They jumped in the water every $1\frac{3}{4}$ hours. How many times did they jump in the water? __3__ times

3. On the same day, Dexter's dad fished for $5\frac{1}{2}$ hours. If he caught a fish every $2\frac{3}{4}$ hours, how many fish did he catch? __2__ fish

4. On the second day, Dexter and Dolly were on the beach for $5\frac{1}{2}$ hours. If they dug a hole every $1\frac{3}{8}$ hours, how many holes did they dig? __4__ holes

5. While Dexter and Dolly were on the beach for $5\frac{3}{5}$ hours, their mom took them a snack every $2\frac{4}{5}$ hours. How many times did she give them a snack? __2__ times

6. On the third day, the family was on the beach for $7\frac{1}{2}$ hours. If they put sunscreen on their noses every $2\frac{1}{2}$ hours, how many times did they use sunscreen? __3__ times

---

Page 97

Checkup 1

Test A (Answers may vary. Possible answers are shown.)

A. $\frac{2}{4}$, $\frac{6}{16}$, $\frac{8}{10}$, $\frac{4}{6}$

B. $\frac{6}{8}$, $\frac{2}{12}$, $\frac{10}{14}$, $\frac{8}{18}$

C. $\frac{14}{20}$, $\frac{10}{12}$

Test B

A. $\frac{5}{6}$, $\frac{1}{4}$, $\frac{5}{8}$, $\frac{1}{3}$

B. $\frac{7}{8}$, $\frac{1}{2}$, $\frac{4}{9}$, $\frac{2}{3}$

C. $\frac{3}{5}$, $\frac{6}{7}$

Page 99

Checkup 2

Test A

A. $\frac{1}{2}$, $\frac{5}{7}$, $\frac{3}{4}$

B. $\frac{3}{5}$, $\frac{2}{5}$, $\frac{1}{3}$

C. $\frac{3}{4}$, 1

D. $\frac{6}{7}$, $\frac{8}{9}$

Test B

A. $\frac{1}{4}$, $\frac{2}{5}$, $\frac{4}{7}$

B. $\frac{3}{5}$, $\frac{1}{3}$, $\frac{2}{3}$

C. $\frac{7}{9}$, $\frac{1}{2}$

D. $\frac{1}{2}$, $\frac{1}{5}$

Page 101

Checkup 3

Test A

A. $\frac{17}{24}$, $\frac{11}{18}$, $\frac{13}{20}$

B. $\frac{3}{4}$, $\frac{16}{21}$, $\frac{7}{15}$

C. $\frac{33}{40}$, $\frac{23}{28}$

D. $\frac{11}{24}$, $\frac{11}{15}$

Test B

A. $\frac{3}{8}$, $\frac{5}{14}$, $\frac{2}{9}$

B. $\frac{3}{10}$, $\frac{1}{6}$, $\frac{23}{42}$

C. $\frac{1}{6}$, $\frac{9}{20}$

D. $\frac{5}{24}$, $\frac{7}{22}$

Page 103
Checkup 4
Test A
A. $5\frac{7}{8}$, $7\frac{5}{7}$, $11\frac{13}{24}$
B. $10\frac{5}{9}$, $6\frac{17}{35}$, $17\frac{2}{3}$
C. $9\frac{17}{36}$, $15\frac{1}{5}$
D. $9\frac{11}{12}$, $11\frac{1}{6}$

Test B
A. $5\frac{1}{4}$, $4\frac{3}{4}$, $2\frac{2}{9}$
B. $6\frac{3}{5}$, $1\frac{1}{6}$, $8\frac{3}{5}$
C. $2\frac{7}{12}$, 1
D. $3\frac{5}{24}$, $7\frac{2}{5}$

Page 105
Checkup 5
Test A
A. $1\frac{1}{2}$, $1\frac{11}{12}$, $\frac{14}{15}$
B. $2\frac{2}{5}$, $1\frac{5}{8}$, $6\frac{17}{21}$
C. $7\frac{5}{8}$, $1\frac{11}{15}$
D. $1\frac{19}{24}$, $7\frac{1}{72}$

Test B
A. $1\frac{7}{8}$, $1\frac{10}{21}$, $3\frac{7}{10}$
B. $4\frac{11}{12}$, $7\frac{7}{12}$, $3\frac{33}{40}$
C. $8\frac{19}{21}$, $2\frac{13}{18}$
D. $4\frac{4}{5}$, $9\frac{1}{2}$

Page 107
Checkup 6
Test A
A. $6\frac{1}{5}$, $2\frac{1}{3}$, $4\frac{7}{8}$
B. $9\frac{4}{5}$, $3\frac{1}{6}$, $10\frac{3}{10}$
C. $7\frac{2}{3}$, $5\frac{7}{9}$
D. $11\frac{1}{4}$, $1\frac{1}{6}$

Test B
A. $3\frac{3}{7}$, $5\frac{7}{8}$, $4\frac{1}{4}$
B. $1\frac{1}{2}$, $10\frac{4}{5}$, $9\frac{2}{3}$
C. $4\frac{3}{14}$, $9\frac{1}{2}$
D. $1\frac{3}{4}$, $7\frac{4}{15}$

Page 109
Checkup 7
Test A
A. $\frac{1}{12}$, $\frac{3}{10}$, $\frac{1}{5}$
B. $\frac{1}{8}$, $\frac{1}{25}$, $\frac{1}{7}$
C. $\frac{3}{14}$, $\frac{2}{27}$
D. $\frac{7}{36}$, $\frac{3}{20}$

Test B
A. $\frac{1}{3}$, $\frac{1}{9}$, $\frac{3}{16}$
B. $\frac{1}{4}$, $\frac{3}{28}$, $\frac{1}{15}$
C. $\frac{7}{15}$, $\frac{3}{10}$
D. $\frac{1}{4}$, $\frac{4}{63}$

Page 111
Checkup 8
Test A
A. $1\frac{2}{3}$, 6, $\frac{3}{4}$
B. $1\frac{1}{3}$, $6\frac{2}{3}$, $\frac{2}{3}$
C. $1\frac{1}{2}$, $\frac{9}{10}$
D. $1\frac{1}{9}$, 3

Test B
A. $\frac{1}{2}$, 3, $\frac{4}{5}$
B. 5, $2\frac{2}{5}$, 1
C. $2\frac{1}{2}$, $3\frac{3}{5}$
D. 3, $2\frac{1}{2}$

Page 113
Checkup 9
Test A
A. $1\frac{4}{15}$, $\frac{7}{8}$
B. $4\frac{7}{12}$, $\frac{31}{35}$
C. $6\frac{9}{28}$, $6\frac{2}{15}$
D. $2\frac{41}{72}$, $1\frac{11}{24}$
E. $\frac{15}{32}$, $6\frac{3}{35}$

Test B
A. $2\frac{16}{45}$, $1\frac{7}{30}$
B. $1\frac{2}{7}$, $2\frac{11}{12}$
C. $5\frac{7}{10}$, $3\frac{1}{12}$
D. $1\frac{29}{60}$, $1\frac{13}{20}$
E. 7, $\frac{19}{56}$

Page 115
Checkup 10
Test A
A. 4, 4, 3
B. $2\frac{1}{2}$, $4\frac{2}{5}$, $3\frac{2}{3}$
C. $7\frac{1}{5}$, $5\frac{1}{10}$
D. 8, $1\frac{1}{2}$

Test B
A. $4\frac{1}{3}$, $6\frac{2}{3}$, $4\frac{1}{5}$
B. 20, $3\frac{1}{4}$, 5
C. $3\frac{9}{10}$, $3\frac{2}{3}$
D. 20, 4

Page 117
Checkup 11
Test A
A. $5\frac{1}{3}$, 7, $4\frac{4}{5}$
B. 12, 12, $3\frac{1}{3}$
C. 9, 16
D. 8, 15

Test B
A. $3\frac{1}{2}$, 22, 8
B. $5\frac{5}{9}$, 24, 15
C. $2\frac{2}{7}$, 18
D. $6\frac{2}{3}$, $9\frac{3}{5}$

Page 119
Checkup 12
Test A
A. $\frac{1}{27}$, $\frac{1}{8}$, $\frac{1}{8}$
B. $\frac{1}{20}$, $\frac{3}{14}$, $\frac{7}{24}$
C. $\frac{5}{42}$, $\frac{3}{50}$
D. $\frac{1}{15}$, $\frac{1}{24}$

Test B
A. $\frac{2}{35}$, $\frac{3}{16}$, $\frac{1}{28}$
B. $\frac{1}{18}$, $\frac{1}{15}$, $\frac{7}{24}$
C. $\frac{1}{36}$, $\frac{1}{9}$
D. $\frac{1}{55}$, $\frac{1}{36}$

Page 121
Checkup 13
Test A
A. $4\frac{1}{2}$, $2\frac{2}{3}$, $1\frac{1}{7}$
B. $\frac{4}{5}$, $\frac{3}{4}$, $\frac{2}{3}$
C. $\frac{5}{6}$, $\frac{24}{25}$
D. $5\frac{3}{5}$, $\frac{49}{60}$

Test B
A. $\frac{35}{36}$, $1\frac{1}{4}$, $\frac{15}{28}$
B. $\frac{25}{36}$, 6, $3\frac{3}{7}$
C. $5\frac{1}{2}$, $\frac{16}{25}$
D. $3\frac{3}{7}$, $2\frac{1}{12}$

Page 123
Checkup 14
Test A
A. $4\frac{1}{6}$, $2\frac{3}{4}$, $\frac{2}{3}$
B. $3\frac{1}{3}$, $4\frac{1}{6}$, $\frac{1}{2}$
C. $2\frac{1}{4}$, 3
D. $\frac{18}{85}$, $\frac{9}{25}$

Text B
A. $4\frac{1}{3}$, 3, 6
B. $2\frac{4}{7}$, $2\frac{2}{3}$, $2\frac{3}{16}$
C. $\frac{16}{39}$, $1\frac{9}{35}$
D. $\frac{3}{4}$, $1\frac{1}{5}$